PROVENCE

TRAVEL GUIDE 2023

The Essence of Provence:
Comprehensive Guide 2023

Silva Martin

DISCLAIMER

The "Provence Travel Guide 2023" provides general information and recommendations for informational purposes only. While we strive for accuracy, we make no warranties about the completeness, reliability, or availability of the information. Travel details may change, so it is essential to verify with relevant authorities before making any arrangements.

Individual preferences may vary, and we do not endorse or guarantee the quality or safety of mentioned establishments or services. Readers should exercise their own judgement and consider personal safety when following suggestions.

We are not liable for any loss, damage, or injury resulting from the use of this guide. It is recommended to consult professional travel advisors and local authorities for specific advice.

External links and references are provided for informational purposes and do not imply endorsement.

Copyrights and intellectual property rights are respected. Please contact us if you believe there is an infringement.

By using this guide, you agree to the above terms and acknowledge your responsibility for your actions.

TABLE OF CONTENTS

10. Day Trips

11. Itineraries

12. Conclusion: Departing with Lasting Memories

Welcome To Provence

Sophia had always been captivated by the charm and beauty of Provence. The picturesque landscapes, vibrant lavender fields, and quaint villages beckoned to her adventurous spirit. Determined to immerse herself in the essence of this enchanting region, she embarked on a solo journey to explore the hidden gems of Provence.

Her adventure began in the historic city of Avignon, where she strolled along the cobblestone streets, marvelling at the well-preserved mediaeval architecture. Sophia couldn't resist the allure of the Palais des Papes, the grand papal palace that dominated the cityscape. As she entered its hallowed halls, she couldn't help but feel the weight of history and the power that once resided within these walls.

Leaving Avignon behind, Sophia embarked on a scenic drive through the countryside, guided by the heady scent of lavender that wafted through the open windows of her car. She found herself in the village of Gordes, perched atop a hill, seemingly frozen in time. The narrow streets led her to an ancient abbey, where she witnessed a breathtaking sunset over the Luberon Valley. The play of colours across the sky painted a *masterpiece that etched itself into Sophia's memory forever.*

Continuing her exploration, Sophia ventured into the charming village of Roussillon, known for its ochre cliffs. The vibrant shades of red, yellow, and orange that adorned the landscape were like an artist's palette come to life. She followed the ochre trail, meandering through the picturesque paths, and couldn't resist dipping her fingers into the richly coloured earth, feeling connected to the very essence of Provence.

Sophia's journey took her to the bustling city of Aix-en-Provence, famous for its artistic heritage. In the footsteps of Cézanne, she wandered through the streets, exploring the vibrant art scene and soaking in the bohemian atmosphere. The Cours Mirabeau, with its elegant fountains and leafy plane trees, became her favourite spot to sit and people-watch, immersing herself in the energy of the city.

To round off her Provence experience, Sophia set out to discover the breathtaking landscapes of the Camargue, a region known for its vast salt marshes and wild horses. She donned her riding boots and embarked on a horseback adventure, trotting through the marshlands, with the flamingos gracefully taking flight in the distance. The unspoiled beauty of this natural wonderland left her in awe of the harmony between humans and nature.

As Sophia's time in Provence drew to a close, she couldn't help but feel transformed by the region's allure. Its vibrant colours, rich history, and the warm hospitality of its people had left an indelible mark on her soul. With a heart full of cherished memories and a deep appreciation for the wonders she had encountered, she bid farewell to Provence, knowing that the spirit of this enchanting place would forever remain in her heart.

Introduction to Provence

Welcome to Provence

Welcome to Provence! Located in southeastern France, Provence is a captivating region known for its natural beauty, rich history, and vibrant culture. Discover breathtaking landscapes of rolling hills, lavender fields, and sparkling coastlines. Immerse yourself in history as you explore ancient ruins and charming villages. Experience the vibrant cultural scene, indulge in exquisite cuisine, and savour world-class wines. Engage in outdoor adventures, from hiking scenic trails to relaxing on sun-kissed beaches. Don't miss the enchanting lavender fields and the coastal gems of Marseille, Cassis, and Saint-Tropez. Provence warmly welcomes you to immerse yourself in its charm and create unforgettable memories.

Why Visit Provence in 2023?

Provence is a compelling destination to visit in 2023 for a variety of reasons. Here's a detailed yet concise overview of why you should consider experiencing Provence this year:

1. Post-Pandemic Rejuvenation: As travel resumes and the world recovers from the pandemic, Provence offers an ideal opportunity for rejuvenation and exploration. The region's serene landscapes, charming villages, and cultural experiences provide a much-needed escape and a chance to reconnect with the world.

2. Captivating Natural Beauty: Provence's natural beauty is truly captivating. From its iconic lavender fields to the stunning coastal scenery, the region offers a picturesque and tranquil setting. In 2023, you can immerse yourself in the breathtaking landscapes and find solace in the region's natural wonders.

3. Rich History and Heritage: Provence is steeped in history and boasts a remarkable cultural

heritage. By visiting in 2023, you can explore ancient Roman ruins, mediaeval castles, and well-preserved historical sites. Uncover the stories of the past and witness the legacy of civilizations that shaped the region.

4. Vibrant Cultural Scene: Provence has a thriving cultural scene that comes alive with festivals, art exhibitions, and traditional events. By visiting in 2023, you can participate in these vibrant celebrations, experiencing the region's unique customs, music, and arts. From renowned music festivals to local traditions, there's always something to celebrate in Provence.

5. Gastronomic Delights: Provence is a culinary paradise, and in 2023, you can indulge in its gastronomic treasures. Discover the flavours of Provençal cuisine, which combines fresh local ingredients, aromatic herbs, and exquisite wines. Immerse yourself in the vibrant food markets, dine in charming bistros, and savour the region's delectable dishes.

6. Outdoor Adventures: Provence offers a wide range of outdoor activities, from hiking and cycling to water sports and leisurely strolls. In 2023, you can take advantage of the region's diverse landscapes, exploring the scenic trails, coastlines, and countryside. Engage in exhilarating adventures and immerse yourself in the natural wonders that Provence has to offer.

7. Authentic Experiences: Visiting Provence in 2023 allows you to experience the region's authentic charm. Interact with the warm and welcoming locals, shop at traditional markets, and explore the lesser-known corners of Provence. Embrace the opportunity to connect with the region's traditions, customs, and way of life.

8. Lavender Blooms: Provence is renowned for its stunning lavender fields, and 2023 is the perfect time to witness this natural spectacle. During the summer months, the fields come alive with vibrant purple blooms, creating a visually stunning landscape and an unforgettable sensory experience.

Visiting Provence in 2023 offers a chance to rediscover the region's beauty, immerse yourself in its rich heritage, and indulge in its delightful offerings. Whether you seek relaxation, cultural exploration, or outdoor adventures, Provence promises a memorable and rewarding experience.

Quick Tips for Travelers

Here are some detailed yet concise quick tips for travellers heading to Provence:

1. Weather and Packing: Check the weather forecast and pack accordingly. Bring lightweight clothing for the warm summers, but also pack layers for cooler evenings. Don't forget essentials like sunscreen, a hat, and comfortable walking shoes.

2. Transportation: Consider renting a car to explore Provence at your own pace. Public transportation options like trains and buses are also available, providing easy access to major cities and towns.

3. Language: While French is the primary language spoken in Provence, English is commonly understood in tourist areas. Learning a few basic French phrases can enhance your experience and help with communication.

4. Local Cuisine: Indulge in the delicious Provençal cuisine. Try regional specialties like bouillabaisse, ratatouille, and fresh seafood. Visit local markets to sample cheeses, olives, and pastries, and enjoy the renowned wines of the region.

5. Cultural Etiquette: Embrace the local customs and etiquette. Greet people with a polite "Bonjour" and follow social norms. Dress modestly when visiting churches or other religious sites.

6. Explore Villages: Don't just focus on the major cities. Discover the charm of Provençal villages like Gordes, Roussillon, and Les Baux-de-Provence. Wander through narrow streets, admire the architecture, and experience the relaxed pace of village life.

7. Lavender Fields: Don't miss the opportunity to visit the iconic lavender fields in Provence. The lavender blooms from June to August, so plan your visit accordingly to witness the stunning purple landscapes.

8. Outdoor Activities: Take advantage of Provence's natural beauty. Go hiking in the Luberon or Verdon Gorge, explore the Calanques along the coast, or enjoy water sports in the Mediterranean Sea.

9. Festivals and Events: Check the local event calendar and see if there are any festivals or events happening during your visit. From music festivals to lavender festivals, these celebrations offer a glimpse into Provençal culture.

10. Slow Down and Enjoy: Provence is known for its laid-back lifestyle, so take the time to relax and soak in the beauty of the region. Enjoy leisurely meals, stroll through vibrant markets, and appreciate the breathtaking landscapes.

Remember to adapt these tips to your own travel preferences and needs. Enjoy your time in Provence and embrace the unique experiences this captivating region has to offer!

Essential Travel Information

Planning Your Trip

Provence, located in southeastern France, is a picturesque region known for its stunning landscapes, rich history, charming villages, and delightful cuisine. Here are some key points to consider when planning your trip to Provence:

1. Best Time to Visit: The best time to visit Provence is during the spring (April to June) and fall (September to October) seasons when the weather is mild, and the region is less crowded with tourists.

2. Duration of Stay: To fully experience Provence, plan to spend at least one week exploring the region. This will allow you to visit popular destinations and also have time to discover hidden gems.

3. Getting There: The main airports serving Provence are Marseille Provence Airport and Nice Côte d'Azur Airport. From there, you can rent a car or use public transportation to reach your desired destinations within the region.

4. Must-Visit Destinations: Provence offers numerous beautiful towns and attractions. Some popular places to visit include:

- Aix-en-Provence: Known for its elegant boulevards, charming squares, and art scene, Aix-en-Provence is a cultural hub with historical sites and vibrant markets.

- Avignon: Famous for the mediaeval Palais des Papes (Papal Palace) and the Pont d'Avignon (Avignon Bridge), this city offers a glimpse into the region's history and is renowned for its annual theatre festival.

- Marseille: As the second-largest city in France, Marseille boasts a vibrant waterfront, diverse culinary scene, and cultural landmarks such as the

Basilique Notre-Dame de la Garde and the historic Le Panier neighbourhood.

   - Gordes: This hilltop village showcases the traditional Provençal architecture and offers breathtaking views of the Luberon Valley. It's a great base for exploring the picturesque countryside.

   - The Calanques: These stunning coastal cliffs and fjord-like inlets are located between Marseille and Cassis, offering opportunities for hiking, swimming, and boat trips.

5. Outdoor Activities: Provence is a paradise for outdoor enthusiasts. Consider activities such as hiking in the Luberon Mountains, cycling through lavender fields in the Plateau de Valensole, or exploring the Verdon Gorge, Europe's deepest canyon.

6. Local Cuisine and Wine: Provence is known for its delicious cuisine and excellent wines. Don't miss trying local specialties like bouillabaisse (a fish stew), ratatouille (a vegetable dish), and pastis

(a traditional anise-flavoured aperitif). Visit vineyards in the Rhône Valley or Côtes de Provence region to sample renowned wines.

7. Practical Tips:
- It's recommended to have a basic understanding of French as English may not be widely spoken in some areas.
- Provence can get quite hot in the summer, so pack sunscreen, hats, and light clothing.
- Consider renting a car to explore the region's smaller villages and countryside.
- Check the schedules of local markets, as they offer fresh produce, local crafts, and a vibrant atmosphere.

Remember to plan your itinerary based on your interests and the experiences you wish to have. Whether it's immersing yourself in the local culture, exploring historical sites, or enjoying the natural beauty, Provence offers a memorable and enriching travel experience.

Visa and Passport Requirements

1. Passport: To travel to Provence, France, you will need a valid passport. Ensure that your passport is valid for at least six months beyond your intended departure date from France.

2. Visa Requirements: The visa requirements for Provence depend on your nationality and the duration of your stay. Citizens of the European Union (EU), European Economic Area (EEA), and Switzerland can travel to Provence and stay for up to 90 days without a visa.

3. Schengen Agreement: France is part of the Schengen Agreement, which allows for free movement within the Schengen Area. Citizens of certain countries, including the United States, Canada, Australia, New Zealand, and many others, can enter France and stay for up to 90 days within a 180-day period without a visa.

4. Visa Exemptions: If you are from a country that is not part of the EU, EEA, or Switzerland, you may need to apply for a Schengen visa before travelling

to Provence. Check with the French embassy or consulate in your country for specific visa requirements and the application process.

5. Visa Application Process: If you require a Schengen visa, you will need to submit an application at the French embassy or consulate in your home country. The application usually requires completing a form, providing supporting documents (such as flight itinerary, accommodation details, travel insurance, proof of financial means), and paying a visa fee. It is advisable to apply well in advance of your planned travel dates.

6. Lengthy Stays or Work: If you plan to stay in Provence for more than 90 days or engage in work or study activities, you may need to apply for a long-stay visa or a specific type of visa or permit. These requirements can vary depending on your circumstances. It is essential to consult the French embassy or consulate in your home country for detailed information and guidance.

7. Travel Insurance: While not mandatory, it is strongly recommended to have travel insurance that covers medical expenses and emergency repatriation during your stay in Provence.

It is crucial to verify the visa and passport requirements specific to your nationality and individual circumstances well in advance of your trip. Contact the French embassy or consulate in your country or visit their official websites for the most up-to-date and accurate information.

Best Time to Visit

The best time to visit Provence, located in southeastern France, is during the spring (April to June) and fall (September to October) seasons. Here's why:

1. Spring (April to June): Spring is a wonderful time to visit Provence. The weather is mild, with pleasant temperatures ranging from 15°C (59°F) to 25°C (77°F). The region comes alive with vibrant colours as flowers bloom, and the countryside is

adorned with lush greenery. It's an ideal time for outdoor activities like hiking, cycling, and exploring the charming villages.

2. Summer (July to August): The summer months in Provence can be quite hot, with temperatures often exceeding 30°C (86°F) and peaking in July and August. While it's the peak tourist season, it can be crowded, especially in popular destinations. However, if you enjoy long sunny days and don't mind the heat, you can still have a delightful time exploring the region's stunning landscapes, coastal areas, and vibrant markets.

3. Fall (September to October): Fall is another fantastic season to visit Provence. The weather remains pleasant, with temperatures ranging from 15°C (59°F) to 25°C (77°F) in September and gradually cooling down in October. The countryside transforms into a tapestry of warm autumn colours, especially in the vineyards and orchards. It's an ideal time to indulge in wine tasting, visit local harvest festivals, and enjoy the region's gastronomic delights.

4. Winter (November to March): Winter in Provence is relatively mild, but the region experiences cooler temperatures and occasional rainfall. While it may not be the best time for outdoor activities, it can still be a great season for exploring historical sites, museums, and enjoying the region's renowned cuisine. The cities and towns are less crowded, and you may find lower prices on accommodations and attractions.

Consider your preferences, activities, and weather conditions when planning your trip to Provence. Keep in mind that the specific timing of seasons may vary slightly from year to year, so it's always a good idea to check the weather forecast and plan accordingly.

Transportation

Provence, located in southeastern France, offers various transportation options to help you explore the region. Here's a detailed and short overview of transportation in Provence:

1. Car Rental: Renting a car is a popular choice for exploring Provence as it provides flexibility and convenience, especially for visiting smaller towns and rural areas. Several car rental companies operate at major airports, train stations, and city centres. Be aware of parking regulations in cities and consider the toll fees on highways.

2. Trains: The train network in Provence is well-developed and offers a convenient way to travel between major cities and towns. The French national railway company, SNCF, operates regular train services connecting Provence with other regions in France. High-speed trains (TGV) serve larger cities like Marseille and Avignon, while regional trains (TER) provide connections to smaller towns.

3. Buses: Bus services are available in Provence, connecting cities, towns, and villages. The regional bus network, operated by companies like Lignes Express Régionales (LER) and Réseau de Transport de la Région Sud (RTS), offers reliable transportation options. Buses are a cost-effective

mode of travel, but they may have limited schedules, especially in rural areas.

4. Local Transportation: Within cities and towns, local transportation options include buses, trams, and taxis. Major cities like Marseille, Aix-en-Provence, and Avignon have comprehensive bus and tram networks, making it easy to navigate urban areas. Taxis are available at taxi stands or can be booked in advance.

5. Cycling: Provence offers beautiful landscapes and cycling-friendly routes, making it an excellent region for cycling enthusiasts. Many towns offer bike rental services, and you can explore scenic countryside roads, vineyards, and coastal paths. Some cities, like Avignon, have bike-sharing programs for short trips within the urban area.

6. Ferries: If you wish to explore the coastal areas of Provence, ferries are available for transportation between ports and islands. For instance, you can take a ferry from Marseille to visit the nearby Frioul Islands or from Toulon to reach the stunning Porquerolles Island.

7. Walking: Provence's charming towns and villages are often best explored on foot. Walking allows you to soak in the local atmosphere, admire historic architecture, and explore narrow streets. Many towns have pedestrianised city centres, making walking a pleasant and enjoyable experience.

It's important to check schedules, purchase tickets in advance when necessary, and be mindful of traffic regulations and parking rules if driving. Public transportation options may have reduced services on Sundays and holidays, so plan your trips accordingly. Consider a combination of transportation modes to optimise your exploration of Provence's diverse landscapes and attractions.

Currency and Money Matters

When visiting Provence, France, it's important to be aware of currency and money-related information. Here's a detailed and short overview:

1. Currency: The official currency of France is the Euro (€). It is widely accepted throughout Provence, including in restaurants, shops, hotels, and tourist attractions. Ensure you have sufficient Euros for your trip.

2. Cash and Cards: Cash is widely used in Provence, especially for small purchases, local markets, and smaller establishments. ATMs are available in cities and towns, allowing you to withdraw cash using your debit or credit card. Major credit cards like Visa, Mastercard, and American Express are widely accepted in most places, but it's advisable to carry some cash for emergencies or smaller establishments that may not accept cards.

3. Exchanging Currency: If you need to exchange currency, it's best to do so at banks or authorised currency exchange offices (bureaux de change). Airports, train stations, and major tourist areas often have currency exchange services, but they may have less favourable rates and higher fees. Compare rates and fees to ensure you get a fair exchange.

4. Tipping: Tipping in France is not mandatory but is appreciated for good service. In restaurants, it is customary to round up the bill or leave a small tip (around 5-10% of the total). If the service charge (service compris) is already included in the bill, additional tipping is not necessary but still appreciated. Tipping for other services, such as taxi rides or hotel staff, is also discretionary.

5. VAT (Value Added Tax): In France, the advertised prices generally include VAT. Non-EU residents may be eligible for a VAT refund on eligible purchases made at participating retailers. Look for stores displaying "Tax-Free Shopping" or "Global Blue" signs and ask for a tax refund form when making qualifying purchases. Follow the necessary procedures to claim your VAT refund at the airport before leaving the EU.

6. Safety and Security: It's advisable to take precautions regarding money and valuables. Keep your cash, cards, and travel documents in a secure place, such as a money belt or a hotel safe. Be cautious of your surroundings and beware of

pickpocketing in crowded tourist areas, public transportation, or busy markets.

7. Currency Conversion: Before your trip, familiarise yourself with the current exchange rates to have an idea of the value of your home currency against the Euro. Online currency converters and smartphone apps can help you calculate approximate conversion rates.

Remember to notify your bank or credit card provider of your travel plans to ensure your cards will work abroad and to avoid any potential disruptions. It's also advisable to carry a mix of payment methods (cash and cards) for convenience and emergencies.

By being prepared and informed about currency and money matters, you can enjoy a smooth and hassle-free experience during your visit to Provence.

Cities and Towns

Marseille: Vibrant Port City

Marseille is a vibrant port city located in the region of Provence in southern France. It is the second-largest city in France after Paris and serves as a major cultural, economic, and transportation hub. Here is some detailed and concise information about Marseille:

1. History: Marseille has a rich and diverse history dating back over 2,600 years. It was founded by the Greeks in 600 BC and has since been influenced by various civilizations, including the Romans, Visigoths, and Moors. Its strategic location as a Mediterranean port has made it a significant trading centre throughout history.

2. Port of Marseille: The city's port, known as the Old Port (Vieux Port), has been the heart of Marseille for centuries. It is a bustling area with fishing boats, yachts, and colourful buildings lining the waterfront. The port remains a vital part

of Marseille's economy and is a popular spot for locals and tourists alike.

3. Cultural Diversity: Marseille is known for its cultural diversity and cosmopolitan atmosphere. The city has been shaped by waves of immigration, particularly from North Africa, which has influenced its cuisine, architecture, and vibrant street life. This multicultural blend is reflected in the diverse neighbourhoods and local markets.

4. Architecture: Marseille boasts a mix of architectural styles due to its long history. The historic centre features narrow, winding streets lined with ancient buildings, while grand 19th-century structures like the Palais Longchamp and Notre-Dame de la Garde add a touch of elegance to the city's skyline. The iconic Cité Radieuse, designed by renowned architect Le Corbusier, is a modernist landmark.

5. Cultural Highlights: The city offers numerous cultural attractions. The MuCEM (Museum of European and Mediterranean Civilizations) showcases the region's heritage, while the

Marseille History Museum delves into the city's past. Marseille is also known for its lively arts scene, with theatres, music venues, and street art contributing to its vibrant cultural tapestry.

6. Culinary Delights: Marseille is a paradise for food lovers. The city is famous for its bouillabaisse, a traditional fish stew, and other Mediterranean delicacies. The lively fish market at the Old Port is a must-visit for seafood enthusiasts, while the neighbourhood of Le Panier offers a charming ambiance with its narrow streets and trendy cafes.

7. Natural Beauty: Marseille is surrounded by stunning natural landscapes. The Calanques, a series of dramatic limestone cliffs and turquoise coves, provide breathtaking hiking and swimming opportunities. The nearby islands of Frioul and Château d'If offer a picturesque escape from the city.

8. Sporting Excellence: Marseille is home to the Stade Vélodrome, one of France's most renowned football stadiums, hosting the city's beloved team, Olympique de Marseille. The city also hosts sailing

events and has been a European Capital of Culture, further emphasising its commitment to sports and the arts.

In summary, Marseille is a vibrant and diverse port city in Provence, France, with a rich history, thriving cultural scene, stunning architecture, and a beautiful natural environment. Its unique blend of influences and its bustling atmosphere make it an exciting destination for travellers.

Aix-en-Provence: Arts and Culture

Aix-en-Provence is a charming city located in the Provence region of southern France. It is renowned for its rich arts and cultural heritage. Here is a detailed yet concise overview of Aix-en-Provence:

1. History: Aix-en-Provence has a history dating back to the Roman era. It was once the capital of Provence and has been a centre for art and learning since the Middle Ages. Its historical streets and

elegant architecture reflect its past as a city of nobility and artistic inspiration.

2. Cours Mirabeau: The Cours Mirabeau is Aix-en-Provence's iconic boulevard, lined with grand mansions, cafés, and fountains. It is a vibrant hub where locals and visitors gather to stroll, relax, and soak in the atmosphere. The avenue has inspired many artists and writers over the centuries.

3. Arts and Culture: Aix-en-Provence is known for its thriving arts and cultural scene. The city has been a source of inspiration for renowned artists like Paul Cézanne, who was born in Aix-en-Provence and left a significant impact on the art world. His former studio, Atelier Cézanne, is now a museum dedicated to his work.

4. Musée Granet: The Musée Granite is Aix-en-Provence's premier art museum, housing an extensive collection of artworks from the 16th century to the present day. It showcases paintings, sculptures, and decorative arts, including works by

renowned artists such as Rembrandt, Van Gogh, and Picasso.

5. Festival d'Aix-en-Provence: Aix-en-Provence is famous for its annual Festival d'Aix-en-Provence, a world-renowned opera and music festival. Established in 1948, the festival brings together acclaimed artists and performers from around the globe, showcasing a diverse range of musical genres and theatrical productions.

6. Historic Old Town: Aix-en-Provence's historic Old Town (Vieil Aix) is a maze of narrow streets, charming squares, and beautiful fountains. It is a delight to explore on foot, with its elegant architecture, artisan boutiques, and bustling markets. The Place de l'Hôtel de Ville and the Place des Prêcheurs are popular gathering spots.

7. Thermal Baths: Aix-en-Provence has a long-standing tradition of thermal baths. The city's natural hot springs have attracted visitors seeking relaxation and wellness for centuries. Les Thermes Sextius is a renowned spa where visitors can indulge in a range of treatments and therapies.

8. Higher Education: Aix-en-Provence is home to several prestigious universities and educational institutions. The most notable is Aix-Marseille University, one of the largest universities in France. The presence of these institutions contributes to the city's vibrant intellectual and cultural atmosphere.

In summary, Aix-en-Provence is a captivating city in Provence, known for its rich artistic heritage, vibrant cultural scene, and architectural beauty. It offers a unique blend of history, arts, and natural beauty that continues to inspire artists and captivate visitors from around the world.

Avignon: The Papal City

Avignon is a historic city located in the Provence region of southern France. It is renowned for its status as the "Papal City" due to its association with the papacy during the 14th century. Here is a detailed yet concise overview of Avignon:

1. Papal History: Avignon gained prominence in the 14th century when it became the residence of the popes, who had temporarily moved from Rome. This period, known as the Avignon Papacy or the Babylonian Captivity, lasted from 1309 to 1377. The popes transformed the city, constructing grand palaces and fortifications.

2. Palais des Papes: The Palais des Papes (Palace of the Popes) is a UNESCO World Heritage Site and the city's most iconic landmark. It is one of the largest and most important mediaeval Gothic buildings in Europe. The palace offers fascinating insights into the papal era, with its opulent chambers, impressive frescoes, and panoramic views from the top.

3. Avignon Bridge: The Pont Saint-Bénézet, also known as the Avignon Bridge, is a famous bridge spanning the Rhône River. Although only four of its original 22 arches remain, it remains an emblematic symbol of the city. The bridge's history and legends are depicted in the well-known folk song "Sur le Pont d'Avignon."

4. Avignon Festival: Avignon is renowned for its annual Avignon Festival (Festival d'Avignon), one of the world's most important contemporary performing arts events. Established in 1947, the festival showcases a diverse range of theatre, dance, music, and visual arts performances, attracting artists and audiences from around the globe.

5. Old Town: Avignon's historic Old Town is a maze of narrow streets, charming squares, and well-preserved mediaeval architecture. The Place de l'Horloge and the Place du Palais are vibrant gathering places filled with restaurants, cafés, and boutiques. Exploring the winding alleys of the Old Town offers a glimpse into the city's mediaeval past.

6. Avignon Ramparts: The city is surrounded by well-preserved mediaeval ramparts, which offer scenic walks and panoramic views. The ramparts provide a glimpse into the city's defensive history and are an excellent vantage point to admire the surrounding countryside.

7. Avignon Cathedral: The Cathedral of
Notre-Dame des Doms is a beautiful Romanesque
and Gothic cathedral located within the Palais des
Papes complex. It houses impressive artworks,
including the famous Virgin Mary statue, and
offers a serene atmosphere for reflection and
prayer.

8. Cuisine and Wine: Avignon is known for its
delicious Provençal cuisine and world-renowned
wines. The city's restaurants and local markets
offer a variety of regional specialties, such as
ratatouille, bouillabaisse, and lavender-infused
desserts. Visitors can also explore nearby
vineyards and indulge in tastings of Côtes du
Rhône wines.

In summary, Avignon is a captivating city in
Provence with a rich history as the Papal City
during the Avignon Papacy. Its architectural
treasures, including the Palais des Papes and the
Avignon Bridge, along with its vibrant arts scene
and culinary delights, make it a must-visit
destination for history enthusiasts, culture lovers,
and food and wine connoisseurs.

Arles: Roman History

Arles is a historic city in the Provence region of southern France that is renowned for its rich Roman history. Here is a detailed yet concise overview of Arles:

1. Roman Heritage: Arles was an important Roman city and a major regional capital during the Roman Empire. Founded in the 1st century BC, it became a flourishing centre of commerce, culture, and politics.

2. Amphitheatre: The Roman amphitheatre in Arles, known as the Arènes d'Arles, is a UNESCO World Heritage Site and one of the city's most iconic landmarks. Built in the 1st century AD, it is one of the best-preserved amphitheatres in the world and could accommodate up to 20,000 spectators for gladiator fights and other public spectacles.

3. Ancient Theatre: Arles boasts an ancient Roman theatre that was constructed around the same time as the amphitheatre. Although partially ruined, it

still offers a glimpse into the grandeur of Roman entertainment. Today, the theatre is occasionally used for cultural events and performances.

4. Roman Baths: The Thermes de Constantin, a set of well-preserved Roman baths, showcases the engineering and architectural prowess of the Romans. Visitors can explore the different rooms, including the caldarium (hot bath) and frigidarium (cold bath), and learn about the Roman bathing rituals.

5. Roman Forum: The Roman Forum in Arles, known as the Cryptoporticus, is an underground gallery that served as a covered walkway and a foundation for buildings. It is an impressive example of Roman engineering and is open for visitors to explore.

6. Alyscamps: The Alyscamps is a Roman necropolis located just outside the city walls of Arles. It was a prestigious burial site during ancient times and is known for its rows of ancient sarcophagi. The site has inspired many artists,

including Vincent van Gogh, who painted several works depicting the Alyscamps.

7. Van Gogh Connection: Arles also has a strong connection to the renowned Dutch painter Vincent van Gogh. Van Gogh spent a significant portion of his artistic career in Arles and created numerous masterpieces inspired by the city's landscapes, architecture, and people. The Van Gogh Foundation in Arles showcases some of his works and provides insights into his time in the city.

8. Historic Centre: Arles' historic centre is a UNESCO World Heritage Site, characterised by its narrow streets, charming squares, and well-preserved mediaeval and Romanesque architecture. The area is filled with museums, art galleries, and picturesque cafés, making it a delightful place to explore.

In summary, Arles is a captivating city in Provence, France, renowned for its Roman history and well-preserved archaeological sites. The Roman amphitheatre, ancient theatre, baths, forum, and necropolis offer a glimpse into the city's grandeur during the Roman era. Additionally, the city's connection to Vincent van Gogh adds an artistic and cultural dimension to its appeal.

Nice: Riviera's Crown Jewel

Nice is a stunning city located on the French Riviera in the Provence-Alpes-Côte d'Azur region of France. Known as the "Riviera's Crown Jewel," Nice offers a unique blend of natural beauty, vibrant culture, and luxurious lifestyle. Here is a detailed yet concise overview of Nice:

1. Promenade des Anglais: The Promenade des Anglais is the iconic seafront promenade that stretches along the Baie des Anges (Bay of Angels). Lined with palm trees, it offers breathtaking views of the Mediterranean Sea and is a popular spot for strolling, jogging, and people-watching.

2. Old Town (Vieux Nice): Nice's Old Town is a charming labyrinth of narrow streets, vibrant squares, and colourful buildings. It exudes a lively

atmosphere with its bustling markets, boutique shops, and traditional restaurants serving local specialties like socca (a chickpea pancake) and pissaladière (a savoury onion tart).

3. Beaches: Nice is famous for its beautiful beaches, making it a sought-after destination for sun-seekers. The city offers both private and public beaches, where visitors can relax on the pebbles or rent a sunbed. The azure waters of the Mediterranean provide a refreshing respite during the summer months.

4. Musée Matisse: Nice is closely associated with the renowned artist Henri Matisse, and the Musée Matisse pays tribute to his work. Located in the leafy Cimiez neighbourhood, the museum showcases a significant collection of his paintings, sculptures, and personal belongings.

5. Promenade du Paillon: The Promenade du Paillon is a beautiful urban park that spans across 12 hectares in the heart of Nice. It offers green spaces, fountains, and play areas, providing a serene oasis in the midst of the city. The park is a

favourite spot for picnics, outdoor activities, and cultural events.

6. Belle Époque Architecture: Nice is known for its impressive Belle Époque architecture, particularly along the Promenade des Anglais and in the Carré d'Or district. These grand buildings with ornate facades and wrought-iron balconies add a touch of elegance and charm to the city's skyline.

7. Museums and Art Galleries: Nice is home to several world-class museums and art galleries. The Musée d'Art Moderne et d'Art Contemporain (MAMAC) showcases contemporary art, while the Musée Marc Chagall exhibits the works of the famous painter. Other notable institutions include the Musée des Beaux-Arts and the Musée d'Art Naïf.

8. Carnival and Festivals: Nice is renowned for its vibrant Carnival, one of the largest and most famous carnivals in the world. The city also hosts numerous festivals throughout the year, celebrating music, film, and cultural diversity. The

lively atmosphere during these events adds to the city's allure.

In summary, Nice is a captivating city on the French Riviera that combines natural beauty, cultural richness, and a luxurious lifestyle. With its stunning promenade, charming Old Town, beautiful beaches, and vibrant arts scene, Nice truly lives up to its reputation as the "Riviera's Crown Jewel" and is a beloved destination for travellers seeking a perfect blend of relaxation and sophistication.

Saint-Tropez: Glamour on the French Riviera

Saint-Tropez is a glamorous coastal town located on the French Riviera in the Provence-Alpes-Côte d'Azur region of France. Renowned for its luxurious lifestyle, stunning beaches, and vibrant nightlife, Saint-Tropez has become a symbol of prestige and elegance. Here is a detailed yet concise overview of Saint-Tropez:

1. Beaches and Coastline: Saint-Tropez is famous for its beautiful beaches and crystal-clear waters. The most well-known beach is Plage de Pampelonne, a long stretch of sandy shoreline that attracts sun-seekers and celebrities from around the world. Other popular beaches include Plage des Salins and Plage de Tahiti.

2. Old Town (La Ponche): The charming Old Town of Saint-Tropez, also known as La Ponche, is a maze of narrow cobblestone streets, historic buildings, and picturesque squares. It retains its old-world charm with colourful houses, quaint shops, and charming cafés. The Vieux Port (Old Port) is a focal point, lined with yachts and fishing boats.

3. Port of Saint-Tropez: The Port of Saint-Tropez is a vibrant hub of activity, filled with luxury yachts and glamorous sailboats. It is a popular spot for strolling, people-watching, and enjoying waterfront dining. The port provides a glamorous backdrop and is an iconic symbol of the town's jet-set lifestyle.

4. Place des Lices: Place des Lices is the main square in Saint-Tropez and a gathering place for locals and visitors alike. It hosts a lively open-air market twice a week, where you can find fresh produce, local delicacies, and stylish clothing. The square is also surrounded by cafés, restaurants, and boutiques.

5. Musée de l'Annonciade: Saint-Tropez is home to the Musée de l'Annonciade, a museum housed in a former chapel. It showcases an impressive collection of modern and contemporary art, with a focus on the renowned Pointillism and Fauvism movements. The museum is a must-visit for art enthusiasts.

6. Nightlife and Entertainment: Saint-Tropez is famous for its vibrant nightlife, attracting international DJs, celebrities, and partygoers. The town boasts exclusive nightclubs, chic bars, and beach clubs where visitors can dance the night away and enjoy the glamorous ambiance.

7. Festivals and Events: Saint-Tropez hosts several exciting festivals and events throughout the year. The most notable is Les Voiles de Saint-Tropez, a prestigious sailing regatta that attracts sailing enthusiasts and spectators. The town also celebrates its maritime heritage with the Bravades de Saint-Tropez, a traditional procession and gun salute.

8. Shopping and Fashion: Saint-Tropez is a shopping paradise, offering a wide range of high-end boutiques, designer stores, and luxury brands. The town has a strong connection to fashion, and visitors can find stylish clothing, accessories, and unique souvenirs in its glamorous shops.

In summary, Saint-Tropez is a glamorous and luxurious destination on the French Riviera, known for its stunning beaches, glamorous lifestyle, and vibrant atmosphere. Whether it's relaxing on the sandy shores, exploring the charming Old Town, or indulging in the town's renowned nightlife, Saint-Tropez offers a perfect blend of glamour, relaxation, and sophistication.

Cannes: Elegance Personified

Cannes is a city located on the French Riviera in the Provence-Alpes-Côte d'Azur region of France. Renowned for its elegance, luxurious lifestyle, and prestigious film festival, Cannes exudes a sophisticated charm. Here is a detailed yet concise overview of Cannes:

1. Cannes Film Festival: Cannes is globally renowned for its prestigious Cannes Film Festival, held annually in May. The festival attracts international film industry professionals, celebrities, and movie enthusiasts from around the world. It showcases a wide range of films, premieres, red carpet events, and awards ceremonies.

2. Promenade de la Croisette: The Promenade de la Croisette in Cannes' iconic seafront boulevard, lined with palm trees and luxury hotels. It offers stunning views of the Mediterranean Sea, exclusive boutiques, upscale restaurants, and beach clubs. The promenade is a favourite spot for leisurely strolls and people-watching.

3. Palais des Festivals et des Congrès: The Palais des Festivals et des Congrès is a prominent landmark in Cannes, serving as the venue for the Cannes Film Festival and other major events. Its striking architecture and red carpet entrance add to the city's allure.

4. Old Town (Le Suquet): Cannes' Old Town, known as Le Suquet, is a charming neighbourhood situated on a hill overlooking the city. It features narrow streets, historic buildings, and a mediaeval castle. Visitors can climb to the top of the hill for panoramic views of Cannes and its surroundings.

5. Luxury Shopping: Cannes is synonymous with luxury shopping. The city boasts a wide array of high-end boutiques and designer stores, particularly along Rue d'Antibes and in the vicinity of the Croisette. Fashion enthusiasts can find renowned international brands and exclusive designer labels.

6. Cannes Marina: Cannes has a modern marina, Port Pierre Canto, which caters to luxury yachts

and boats. It offers a glimpse into the opulent lifestyle associated with the city and provides a picturesque setting for waterfront dining and relaxation.

7. Museums and Cultural Heritage: Cannes is home to several museums and cultural attractions. The Musée de la Castre houses a diverse collection of art, artefacts, and archaeological objects, while the Musée de la Mer showcases marine life and maritime history. The Villa Domergue is a stunning mansion with beautiful gardens that hosts art exhibitions and cultural events.

8. Beaches and Waterfront Activities: Cannes offers pristine sandy beaches, including Plage de la Croisette and Plage du Midi, where visitors can bask in the sun and enjoy water sports. The city also offers boat tours, sailing excursions, and yacht charters for those seeking a nautical experience.

In summary, Cannes epitomises elegance and sophistication on the French Riviera. With its renowned film festival, stunning seafront promenade, luxurious shopping, and cultural attractions, Cannes offers a blend of glamour, cultural richness, and a luxurious lifestyle that appeals to visitors from around the world.

Nimes: Ancient Wonders and Modern Charms

Nîmes is a city in the Provence region of southern France known for its ancient wonders and modern charms. Here is a detailed yet concise overview of Nîmes:

1. Roman Amphitheatre: The Arena of Nîmes, also known as the Nîmes Amphitheatre, is a well-preserved Roman arena that dates back to the 1st century AD. It is one of the best-preserved amphitheatres in the world and is still used today for various events, including bullfights and concerts.

2. Maison Carrée: The Maison Carrée is a remarkably preserved Roman temple in Nîmes.

Built in the 1st century BC, it is considered one of the best-preserved Roman temples anywhere. Today, it serves as a museum and showcases exhibitions on Nîmes' history and culture.

3. Pont du Gard: Located near Nîmes, the Pont du Gard is a magnificent Roman aqueduct and a UNESCO World Heritage Site. It was built in the 1st century AD and spans the Gardon River. The bridge stands as a testament to Roman engineering and is a popular tourist attraction.

4. Jardins de la Fontaine: The Jardins de la Fontaine is a beautiful park located in the heart of Nîmes. It features landscaped gardens, fountains, and the Temple of Diana. The park is a peaceful oasis and offers a perfect place for a leisurely stroll or a picnic.

5. Nîmes Cathedral: The Nîmes Cathedral, also known as the Cathédrale Notre-Dame-et-Saint-Castor de Nîmes, is a stunning example of Gothic architecture. Built between the 11th and 14th centuries, the cathedral

boasts intricate stained glass windows and a grand organ.

6. Carré d'Art: Carré d'Art is a modern art museum in Nîmes designed by renowned architect Norman Foster. It houses a diverse collection of contemporary art and hosts temporary exhibitions, making it a vibrant centre for art enthusiasts.

7. Old Town: Nîmes' Old Town is a charming area with narrow streets, historic buildings, and lively squares. It is home to shops, boutiques, cafés, and restaurants where visitors can experience the local ambiance and savour the regional cuisine.

8. Feria de Nîmes: Nîmes is known for its lively festivals, particularly the Feria de Nîmes, a traditional celebration held twice a year. During Feria, the city comes alive with bullfights, street parties, music, and colourful parades, showcasing the rich cultural heritage of the region.

In summary, Nîmes is a captivating city in Provence with a rich historical heritage. Its ancient

Roman monuments, such as the Arena, Maison Carrée, and Pont du Gard, are extraordinary reminders of its past. Alongside these ancient wonders, Nîmes offers modern attractions, vibrant festivals, and a charming Old Town, making it a delightful destination that blends ancient history with modern charm.

Toulon: Sun, Sea, and Beauty

Toulon is a beautiful city located on the coast of the Provence-Alpes-Côte d'Azur region in southern France. Known for its sun, sea, and natural beauty, Toulon offers a delightful combination of coastal charm, historic sites, and picturesque landscapes. Here is a detailed yet concise overview of Toulon:

1. Old Town (Le Mourillon): Toulon's Old Town, known as Le Mourillon, is a lively neighbourhood with narrow streets, colourful facades, and charming squares. It offers a pleasant atmosphere for strolling, exploring local shops, and enjoying

traditional Provencal cuisine in its many restaurants and cafés.

2. Toulon Harbor: Toulon is home to a bustling harbour that serves as a naval base and a picturesque waterfront area. Visitors can admire the array of boats and ships, enjoy waterfront dining, or take a boat tour to explore the stunning coastline and nearby islands.

3. Mount Faron: Mount Faron is a prominent mountain that overlooks Toulon, offering breathtaking panoramic views of the city and the Mediterranean Sea. Visitors can reach the summit by car, cable car, or on foot, and explore the stunning natural landscapes and hiking trails.

4. Musée National de la Marine: The Musée National de la Marine in Toulon is a naval museum that showcases the maritime history of the city and the French Navy. It features exhibitions on shipbuilding, navigation, and maritime artefacts, providing a fascinating insight into Toulon's naval heritage.

5. Plages du Mourillon: Toulon boasts beautiful beaches, particularly in the Mourillon district. The Plages du Mourillon offer sandy shores, clear blue waters, and a range of beachfront amenities. Visitors can relax under the sun, engage in water sports, or enjoy a leisurely seaside stroll.

6. Place de la Liberté: Place de la Liberté is a vibrant square in the heart of Toulon, surrounded by elegant buildings and bustling shops. It serves as a meeting point and hosts various events, including markets, concerts, and festivals throughout the year.

7. Mont Faron Zoo: Located on Mont Faron, the Mont Faron Zoo is a popular attraction in Toulon. It is home to a diverse range of animals, including big cats, primates, and reptiles. Visitors can enjoy a scenic visit to the zoo while taking in the beautiful natural surroundings.

8. Provençal Markets: Toulon offers a selection of vibrant Provençal markets where visitors can immerse themselves in the local culture and sample regional produce. The Cours Lafayette

market is particularly renowned for its fresh fruits, vegetables, spices, and traditional Provençal products.

In summary, Toulon is a sun-soaked coastal city in Provence that combines natural beauty, maritime heritage, and a relaxed Mediterranean ambiance. With its charming Old Town, picturesque harbour, stunning mountain views, and inviting beaches, Toulon offers a delightful experience for visitors seeking sun, sea, and the beauty of southern France.

Cassis: Coastal Charm and Calanques

Cassis is a picturesque coastal town located in the Provence-Alpes-Côte d'Azur region of France. Known for its coastal charm, stunning calanques (inlets), and vibrant harbour, Cassis offers a serene and idyllic setting. Here is a detailed yet concise overview of Cassis:

1. Calanques National Park: Cassis is situated at the gateway to the Calanques National Park, a natural reserve renowned for its breathtaking limestone cliffs, turquoise waters, and hidden calanques. Visitors can explore the park by hiking along the well-marked trails or taking boat tours to discover the stunning beauty of the calanques.

2. Port and Old Town: The picturesque port of Cassis is the heart of the town, lined with colourful buildings, charming cafes, and waterfront restaurants. Visitors can enjoy a leisurely stroll along the quay, watch the fishing boats, and savour fresh seafood while taking in the relaxed Mediterranean atmosphere.

3. Cassis Beaches: Cassis boasts several beautiful beaches where visitors can unwind and soak up the sun. The main beach, Plage de la Grande Mer, offers a sandy shore and clear waters, while smaller beaches like Plage du Bestouan and Plage de l'Arène offer a more secluded and tranquil setting.

4. Cassis Vineyards: The region around Cassis is known for its vineyards, particularly its white wines. Visitors can explore the local vineyards, taste the renowned Cassis wines, and learn about the winemaking process. The vineyards offer a scenic backdrop of rolling hills and lush greenery.

5. Cap Canaille: Cap Canaille is a stunning cliff located near Cassis and is the highest sea cliff in France. Visitors can drive or hike to the top for panoramic views of the Mediterranean coastline and the picturesque town of Cassis.

6. Provençal Market: Cassis hosts a lively Provençal market where visitors can immerse themselves in the vibrant local atmosphere. The market offers a variety of fresh produce, regional specialties, handicrafts, and souvenirs.

7. Water Activities: Cassis is a haven for water sports enthusiasts. Visitors can enjoy activities such as kayaking, paddleboarding, and snorkelling in the clear waters of the Mediterranean. Boat trips and cruises are also available for those who want to explore the coastline and calanques.

8. Cassis Festivals: Cassis hosts several festivals throughout the year, celebrating local traditions, culture, and gastronomy. The Cassis Wine Festival, held in September, is a popular event that showcases the region's wines and offers tastings, music, and entertainment.

In summary, Cassis is a charming coastal town in Provence that captivates visitors with its coastal beauty, stunning calanques, and relaxed Mediterranean ambiance. Whether exploring the natural wonders of the Calanques National Park, enjoying the picturesque harbour, or indulging in the local gastronomy, Cassis offers a delightful experience of coastal charm in the heart of Provence.

Natural Wonders

Lavender Fields: Fragrant Paradise

Lavender Fields: Fragrant Paradise in Provence is a renowned tourist attraction located in the Provence region of southeastern France. This stunning natural landscape is characterised by vast fields of lavender plants, creating a captivating sight and emitting a delightful fragrance that has enchanted visitors for centuries.

Key points about Lavender Fields: Fragrant Paradise in Provence:

1. Location: The Lavender Fields are primarily found in the Plateau de Valensole, a picturesque area located in the Alpes-de-Haute-Provence department of Provence, France. The region is known for its favourable climate and fertile soil, which make it ideal for cultivating lavender.

2. Lavender Varieties: The Lavender Fields in Provence primarily feature two main lavender varieties: Lavandula angustifolia (true lavender) and Lavandula x intermedia (lavandin). These varieties have distinct characteristics, including differences in size, colour, and fragrance.

3. Blooming Season: The lavender plants in Provence typically bloom from June to August, reaching their peak in July. During this time, the fields transform into vibrant expanses of purple, creating a mesmerising visual spectacle.

4. Scenic Beauty: The Lavender Fields offer breathtaking landscapes that stretch as far as the eye can see. The undulating hills covered in rows of lavender create a patchwork of colours and textures, attracting visitors from all over the world.

5. Fragrance and Aromatherapy: Lavender is renowned for its aromatic properties, and the Lavender Fields in Provence provide an immersive sensory experience. The air is filled with the soothing scent of lavender, creating a calming and

therapeutic atmosphere that promotes relaxation and well-being.

6. Photography and Art: The Lavender Fields in Provence have become an iconic subject for photographers and artists. The vibrant hues, contrasting landscapes, and symmetrical patterns make for stunning visual compositions, inspiring countless works of art.

7. Local Products and Traditions: The cultivation of lavender has deep roots in Provence's cultural heritage. The region is known for its production of lavender-related products, such as essential oils, soaps, perfumes, and culinary ingredients. Visitors can explore local markets and shops to purchase these authentic lavender goods.

8. Tourism and Activities: The Lavender Fields attract a significant number of tourists each year, especially during the blooming season. Visitors can take guided tours, walk through the fields, and learn about the cultivation and harvesting processes. Additionally, various lavender festivals and events are held in nearby towns, celebrating

the beauty and cultural significance of lavender in the region.

The Lavender Fields: Fragrant Paradise in Provence provide an enchanting and sensory-rich experience, allowing visitors to immerse themselves in the beauty and aroma of this captivating landscape.

The Verdon Gorge: Nature's Masterpiece

The Verdon Gorge, often referred to as "Nature's Masterpiece in Provence," is a breathtaking natural wonder located in the Provence-Alpes-Côte d'Azur region of southeastern France. Known for its stunning turquoise-coloured waters and dramatic limestone cliffs, it is considered one of Europe's most beautiful river canyons.

Key points about The Verdon Gorge: Nature's Masterpiece in Provence:

1. Location: The Verdon Gorge is situated in the Verdon Natural Regional Park, spanning across the departments of Alpes-de-Haute-Provence and Var. It is named after the Verdon River, which flows through the gorge, carving its way through the limestone over millions of years.

2. Geological Formation: The Verdon Gorge was formed through the erosive action of the Verdon River, which created the deep and narrow canyon over time. The white limestone cliffs that tower over the turquoise waters provide a striking contrast and contribute to the gorge's awe-inspiring beauty.

3. Scenic Beauty: The Verdon Gorge offers breathtaking vistas and panoramic views at every turn. The crystal-clear waters of the Verdon River are renowned for their striking turquoise colour, which is a result of sunlight reflecting off the limestone bedrock. The steep cliffs, some reaching heights of over 700 metres (2,300 feet), create a dramatic and awe-inspiring landscape.

4. Outdoor Activities: The Verdon Gorge is a paradise for outdoor enthusiasts and adventure seekers. Visitors can engage in a variety of activities, including hiking, rock climbing, kayaking, canoeing, and even paragliding. The gorge's rugged terrain and pristine waters provide opportunities for unforgettable experiences and exploration.

5. Verdon Gorge Road: The scenic Verdon Gorge Road, officially known as the Corniche Sublime, offers a stunning drive along the edge of the canyon. This winding road provides numerous viewpoints and overlooks, allowing travellers to admire the gorge's grandeur and capture breathtaking photographs.

6. Lac de Sainte-Croix: The Verdon Gorge is home to the picturesque Lac de Sainte-Croix, a turquoise reservoir located at the entrance of the canyon. The lake offers opportunities for swimming, boating, and relaxing on its sandy beaches. It serves as a popular spot for water sports and leisure activities.

7. Flora and Fauna: The Verdon Gorge is a haven for diverse flora and fauna. The surrounding areas are covered with lush vegetation, including oak and pine forests, as well as Mediterranean scrubland. Visitors may encounter various bird species, butterflies, and even eagles soaring above the cliffs.

The Verdon Gorge: Nature's Masterpiece in Provence is a natural wonder that leaves visitors awe-struck with its striking beauty and opportunities for outdoor adventure. Whether exploring the canyon by foot, water, or car, it offers an unforgettable experience in the heart of Provence.

Calanques National Park: Land Meets Sea

Calanques National Park is a stunning natural park located along the Mediterranean coast in the Provence-Alpes-Côte d'Azur region of southern France. Known as "Land Meets Sea in Provence," it is renowned for its rugged limestone cliffs, turquoise waters, and picturesque calanques.

Key points about Calanques National Park: Land Meets Sea in Provence:

1. Location: Calanques National Park stretches along the coastline between the cities of Marseille and Cassis, covering approximately 20 kilometres (12 miles) of stunning Mediterranean landscape. It is easily accessible from both cities, making it a popular destination for locals and tourists alike.

2. Geological Features: The park's most notable features are its calanques, which are narrow, steep-walled inlets carved into the limestone cliffs by the sea over millions of years. These calanques create a breathtaking contrast between the deep blue waters and the towering white cliffs, offering a unique and picturesque coastal scenery.

3. Biodiversity and Endangered Species: Calanques National Park is recognized for its rich biodiversity and serves as a sanctuary for various plant and animal species. It is home to over 900 plant

species, including rare and endemic ones. The park also provides a habitat for endangered species such as the Bonelli's eagle and the Mediterranean monk seal.

4. Hiking and Outdoor Activities: The park offers a plethora of outdoor activities for nature enthusiasts. Visitors can explore the park's numerous hiking trails that wind through the rugged terrain, offering stunning views of the calanques and the Mediterranean Sea. The crystal-clear waters also provide opportunities for swimming, snorkelling, and diving.

5. Cultural Heritage: Calanques National Park is not only a natural treasure but also a place of cultural significance. The park's coastal areas have been inhabited for thousands of years, and remnants of ancient settlements, including prehistoric caves and Roman ruins, can be found throughout the park, adding an extra layer of historical interest.

6. Protection and Conservation: Calanques National Park was established in 2012 to protect

and preserve the fragile coastal ecosystem. The park's regulations aim to balance the conservation of its natural and cultural heritage with sustainable tourism and recreational activities. Visitors are encouraged to follow guidelines to minimise their impact on the environment.

7. Boat Tours: Exploring the park by boat is a popular way to experience the beauty of the calanques up close. Boat tours depart from Marseille and Cassis, taking visitors on scenic cruises through the narrow inlets, allowing them to admire the towering cliffs, hidden beaches, and clear waters.

Calanques National Park: Land Meets Sea in Provence offers a unique blend of breathtaking natural beauty, outdoor activities, and cultural heritage. Whether hiking the trails, swimming in the pristine waters, or simply marvelling at the coastal scenery, visitors are sure to be captivated by the park's charm and tranquillity.

Camargue: Unique Wildlife Sanctuary

Camargue, located in the Provence region of southern France, is a unique wildlife sanctuary renowned for its diverse ecosystems and abundant wildlife. It is a captivating destination known for its picturesque landscapes, marshes, salt flats, and the iconic Camargue horses and pink flamingos.

Key points about Camargue: Unique Wildlife Sanctuary in Provence:

1. Location and Geography: Camargue is located in the delta of the Rhône River, stretching along the Mediterranean coast. It covers an area of approximately 930 square kilometres (360 square miles) and is characterised by a mix of lagoons, marshes, salt flats, and vast expanses of wetlands.

2. Biodiversity and Wildlife: Camargue is home to a remarkable variety of flora and fauna, making it a haven for wildlife enthusiasts. It is known for its iconic white Camargue horses, which roam freely

across the marshlands. The region is also a significant nesting site for numerous bird species, including pink flamingos, herons, and various migratory birds.

3. Flamingos: The pink flamingos are among the most famous and iconic inhabitants of Camargue. They gather in large flocks, creating a stunning sight with their vibrant pink plumage. The salt flats and lagoons provide the perfect habitat for these graceful birds.

4. Wetland Ecosystem: The wetlands of Camargue are of great ecological importance. The salt marshes and lagoons are vital for water purification and act as breeding grounds for a variety of fish and crustaceans. They also support a diverse array of plant species, including salt-resistant vegetation like sea lavender and glasswort.

5. Rice Fields and Agriculture: Camargue is known for its rice cultivation, with the region being a major producer of high-quality rice in France. The fertile soil and ample water supply from the Rhône

River make it an ideal location for rice farming. Visitors can explore the vast rice fields, learn about the cultivation process, and sample delicious local rice-based dishes.

6. Nature Reserves and Conservation: Several nature reserves and protected areas have been established in Camargue to safeguard its unique ecosystems and wildlife. These reserves provide a sanctuary for various species and contribute to the preservation of the region's natural heritage.

7. Traditional Culture: Camargue has a rich cultural heritage deeply rooted in its rural traditions. The local population includes Camarguais, a distinct group known for their customs, costumes, and traditional bullfighting events. Visitors can experience the traditional lifestyle and witness bull games and equestrian spectacles unique to the region.

Camargue: Unique Wildlife Sanctuary in Provence offers a captivating blend of stunning landscapes, abundant wildlife, and cultural richness. From observing flamingos and wild horses to exploring the wetlands and experiencing local traditions, visitors are immersed in a truly unique and enchanting environment.

The Luberon: Scenic Splendour and Villages

The Luberon is a region in Provence, France, known for its scenic splendour and charming villages. Nestled between the Alpes-de-Haute-Provence and Vaucluse departments, the Luberon offers a captivating blend of natural beauty, picturesque landscapes, and historic villages.

Key points about The Luberon: Scenic Splendour and Villages in Provence:

1. Location: The Luberon region is located in southeastern France, within the Provence-Alpes-Côte d'Azur région. It stretches between the towns of Apt and Cavaillon and is

easily accessible from major cities like Avignon and Marseille.

2. Natural Beauty: The Luberon is renowned for its diverse and breathtaking landscapes. It features rolling hills, vineyards, orchards, and extensive fields of lavender and sunflowers. The region is also home to the Luberon Massif, a small mountain range offering stunning views and opportunities for hiking and outdoor activities.

3. Charming Villages: The Luberon is dotted with enchanting villages that exude a timeless beauty and charm. Some of the most notable villages include Gordes, Roussillon, Bonnieux, Ménerbes, and Lourmarin. These villages showcase traditional Provençal architecture, narrow cobblestone streets, ancient churches, and picturesque squares.

4. Cultural and Historical Significance: The Luberon region has a rich historical and cultural heritage. Many of the villages boast ancient castles, forts, and mediaeval churches that provide a glimpse into the region's past. The area has also

attracted artists, writers, and musicians, who draw inspiration from its scenic landscapes and vibrant culture.

5. Lavender Fields and Provençal Markets: The Luberon is renowned for its lavender fields, particularly around the village of Sault. The blooming lavender fields offer a visual feast and a captivating fragrance. The region is also known for its vibrant Provençal markets, where visitors can immerse themselves in the local culture, taste regional delicacies, and browse a variety of crafts, textiles, and fresh produce.

6. Outdoor Activities: The Luberon is an outdoor enthusiast's paradise, offering numerous activities for nature lovers. Visitors can explore the region on foot or by bicycle, following the well-marked trails that crisscross the countryside. The Luberon Regional Nature Park is an excellent destination for hiking, picnicking, and birdwatching.

7. Wine and Gastronomy: The Luberon is part of the Provence wine region, renowned for its rosé wines. Wine enthusiasts can visit vineyards and

wineries to taste and learn about the local wines. The region also boasts a vibrant gastronomy scene, with traditional Provençal cuisine that highlights fresh local ingredients such as olives, herbs, and seasonal produce.

The Luberon: Scenic Splendour and Villages in Provence offers a perfect blend of natural beauty, cultural heritage, and rural charm. With its picturesque villages, stunning landscapes, outdoor activities, and delectable cuisine, the Luberon region invites visitors to immerse themselves in the splendours of Provence.

Provencal Culture and History

Provencal Cuisine: Gastronomic Delight

Provencal cuisine refers to the traditional culinary traditions of the Provence region in southeastern France. It is known for its rich flavours, vibrant colours, and fresh ingredients, which are often sourced from the Mediterranean climate and fertile lands of the region. Provencal cuisine is considered one of the finest and most diverse regional cuisines in France, offering a gastronomic delight for food enthusiasts.

Key Characteristics of Provencal Cuisine:

1. Fresh Ingredients: Provencal cuisine relies heavily on fresh, seasonal produce. Fruits, vegetables, herbs, and aromatic spices play a significant role in the flavour profile of dishes.

2. Mediterranean Influence: The region's proximity to the Mediterranean Sea greatly influences Provencal cuisine. Olive oil, garlic, tomatoes, peppers, and other Mediterranean ingredients are commonly used.

3. Herbs and Aromatics: Provence is known for its fragrant herbs, such as rosemary, thyme, oregano, and lavender. These herbs add distinct flavours and aromas to dishes, enhancing their taste.

4. Seafood: Being located along the coast, seafood is an essential part of Provencal cuisine. Fresh fish, shellfish, and other seafood varieties are incorporated into various dishes, such as bouillabaisse (a traditional fish stew).

5. Regional Specialties: Provence boasts a range of regional specialties that have gained international recognition. Some popular dishes include ratatouille (a vegetable stew), socca (a chickpea flour pancake), aioli (a garlic-infused mayonnaise), and tapenade (a paste made from olives and capers).

6. Local Cheeses: Provence is home to several renowned cheeses, including Banon, Pélardon, and Tomme de Provence. These cheeses are often enjoyed as standalone treats or used in dishes like salads and gratins.

7. Wines and Rosé: Provence is celebrated for its wine production, especially its refreshing rosé wines. The region's vineyards produce a variety of red, white, and rosé wines that pair perfectly with Provencal cuisine.

8. Provençal Market Culture: Provence is famous for its vibrant open-air markets, where locals and tourists can find a wide array of fresh produce, cheeses, meats, and other culinary delights. These markets are an integral part of the food culture and offer an opportunity to experience the region's gastronomy firsthand.

Overall, Provencal cuisine combines the rustic flavours of the countryside with the fresh bounties of the Mediterranean, resulting in a delightful culinary experience. It reflects the region's rich history, cultural diversity, and strong connection to the land and sea. Whether you're savouring a traditional Provençal dish or exploring the local markets, Provence offers an unforgettable gastronomic journey.

Wine Tasting: Vinicultural Journey

Wine tasting in Provence offers a vinicultural journey that combines centuries of winemaking tradition with the breathtaking landscapes of the region. Here's a detailed yet concise overview of the experience:

1. Vineyards and Terroir: Provence is home to a diverse range of vineyards that benefit from the region's Mediterranean climate, abundant sunshine, and varied terroir. The terroir includes different soil types, altitudes, and microclimates, which contribute to the unique characteristics of the wines produced.

2. Grape Varieties: Provence is primarily known for its production of rosé wines, which account for a significant portion of the region's output. The main grape varieties used for rosé include Grenache, Syrah, Cinsault, Mourvèdre, and Carignan. In addition to rosé, Provence also produces red and white wines using grape varieties such as Grenache, Syrah, Mourvèdre, and Vermentino.

3. Wine Tasting Experiences: Numerous wineries and vineyards in Provence welcome visitors for wine tasting experiences. These establishments often offer guided tours, allowing visitors to explore the vineyards, learn about the winemaking process, and discover the history and traditions of the region.

4. Provencal Rosé: Provence is renowned for its exceptional rosé wines. The region's rosés are typically dry, crisp, and refreshing, with delicate flavours of red fruits, citrus, and floral notes. Wine enthusiasts can enjoy sampling different styles of rosé, ranging from pale pink to deeper hues, and savour the distinct characteristics imparted by

various grape varieties and winemaking techniques.

5. Food and Wine Pairing: Provence's gastronomy is intertwined with its wines, and wine tasting often incorporates food pairings. The region's cuisine, with its emphasis on fresh, local ingredients, pairs wonderfully with the local wines. From seafood and grilled meats to aromatic herbs and flavorful cheeses, there are endless opportunities to explore the delightful combinations of Provencal wines and dishes.

6. Wine Festivals and Events: Provence hosts various wine festivals and events throughout the year, providing an immersive experience for wine enthusiasts. These festivals offer opportunities to taste a wide selection of wines, meet winemakers, participate in educational workshops, and celebrate the region's vinicultural heritage.

7. Scenic Vineyard Landscapes: Wine tasting in Provence is not only about the wines themselves but also about the stunning landscapes that surround the vineyards. The region boasts

picturesque countryside, rolling hills, lavender fields, and charming villages, creating a serene backdrop for wine enthusiasts to indulge in their vinicultural journey.

8. Sustainable and Organic Practices: Many wineries in Provence have embraced sustainable and organic winemaking practices, prioritising environmental stewardship and the production of high-quality wines. Visitors can learn about these practices and gain insights into the commitment of winemakers towards preserving the natural beauty and resources of the region.

Wine tasting in Provence offers an immersive and enriching experience, allowing visitors to delve into the world of fine wines, appreciate the region's cultural heritage, and soak in the natural beauty that makes Provence a remarkable destination for wine lovers.

Roman Heritage: Arles, Orange, Pont du Gard

Arles, Orange, and Pont du Gard in Provence are significant sites that showcase the rich Roman heritage of the region. Here's a detailed yet concise overview of each:

1. Arles:
Arles, located on the banks of the Rhône River, boasts an impressive Roman history. The city's Roman monuments, collectively known as the Arles Roman and Romanesque Monuments, have been designated as a UNESCO World Heritage site. Key attractions include:

- Amphitheatre: The Roman amphitheatre, built in the 1st century AD, is one of the best-preserved amphitheatres in the world. It could hold up to 20,000 spectators and was used for gladiatorial contests and other public spectacles.

- Theatre: The ancient Roman theatre, constructed during the 1st century BC, is renowned for its well-preserved stage wall and seating area. It continues to host cultural events and performances to this day.

- Alyscamps: This ancient Roman necropolis is a site of significant historical and artistic importance. It features rows of sarcophagi and served as a burial ground during the Roman period.

2. Orange:
Orange, a city in the Vaucluse department of Provence, is home to one of the most exceptional Roman structures in France:

- Roman Theatre of Orange: This incredibly well-preserved Roman theatre, built in the 1st century AD, is an UNESCO World Heritage site. It is renowned for its monumental stage wall, which stands almost intact, as well as its seating area. The theatre is still used for various cultural events, including the renowned Chorégies d'Orange opera festival.

3. Pont du Gard:

The Pont du Gard, located near the town of Vers-Pont-du-Gard, is an ancient Roman aqueduct and bridge that stands as a testament to Roman engineering marvels:

- Aqueduct and Bridge: The Pont du Gard, constructed in the 1st century AD, served as an aqueduct that transported water over 50 kilometres to the city of Nemausus (modern-day Nîmes). The three-tiered structure, built without the use of mortar, stands at an impressive height of 49 metres and is considered a masterpiece of ancient engineering.

Visiting these Roman heritage sites in Provence offers a unique opportunity to step back in time and experience the grandeur of the Roman Empire. The architectural splendour, historical significance, and cultural value of these sites highlight the enduring legacy of the Romans in the region.

Aix-en-Provence: Birthplace of Cézanne

Aix-en-Provence, known as the birthplace of renowned artist Paul Cézanne, is a charming city in Provence, France. Here's a detailed yet concise overview of Aix-en-Provence:

1. Birthplace of Paul Cézanne: Aix-en-Provence holds great significance in the art world as the birthplace and hometown of post-impressionist painter Paul Cézanne (1839-1906). Cézanne is considered one of the most influential artists of the 19th and early 20th centuries, known for his innovative approach to form and colour.

2. Cézanne's Influence: Aix-en-Provence had a profound impact on Cézanne's artistic development. The city's landscapes, including the Montagne Sainte-Victoire, served as inspiration for many of his iconic paintings. Cézanne's use of light, colour, and geometric shapes captured the essence of Provence and left an indelible mark on the art world.

3. Cézanne's Studio: Visitors to Aix-en-Provence can explore Cézanne's former studio, known as the Atelier Cézanne. Preserved as a museum, it offers an intimate look into the artist's working environment. The studio provides insight into Cézanne's artistic process and displays some of his personal belongings.

4. Old Town: Aix-en-Provence features a picturesque old town characterised by narrow, winding streets, charming squares, and beautiful architecture. The city's historic centre is lined with elegant mansions, fountains, and vibrant markets. The Cours Mirabeau, a famous avenue flanked by plane trees, is a popular spot for strolling and people-watching.

5. Cultural Heritage: Aix-en-Provence is rich in cultural heritage. It is home to several impressive landmarks, including the Cathédrale Saint-Sauveur, a stunning mediaeval cathedral with a mix of architectural styles, and the Hôtel de Ville, a magnificent town hall. The city also hosts various cultural events, such as the prestigious

Aix-en-Provence Festival, known for its opera and classical music performances.

6. Markets and Cuisine: Aix-en-Provence's markets are renowned for their vibrant atmosphere and diverse offerings. The main market, the Marché d'Aix-en-Provence, is a must-visit, featuring an array of fresh produce, local delicacies, and artisanal products. The city's culinary scene is equally enticing, with numerous restaurants and cafés serving up traditional Provençal cuisine.

7. Higher Education and Vibrant Student Life: Aix-en-Provence is home to several prestigious universities, including Aix-Marseille University. The city's vibrant student population adds to its lively atmosphere, with a plethora of cultural activities, nightlife options, and a thriving arts scene.

Aix-en-Provence's connection to Paul Cézanne, its captivating old town, cultural heritage, and vibrant ambiance make it an enchanting destination for art lovers, history enthusiasts, and those seeking the quintessential charm of Provence.

Van Gogh's Footsteps: Saint-Rémy-de-Provence

Saint-Rémy-de-Provence, located in the heart of Provence, holds great significance in the life and artistic journey of Vincent van Gogh. Here's a detailed yet concise overview of Van Gogh's footsteps in Saint-Rémy-de-Provence:

1. Van Gogh's Residence: Van Gogh voluntarily admitted himself to the Saint-Paul-de-Mausole asylum in Saint-Rémy-de-Provence in 1889. He spent a year at the asylum, during which he produced some of his most iconic and celebrated works.

2. Inspiration in Nature: The beautiful landscapes surrounding Saint-Rémy-de-Provence provided Van Gogh with abundant inspiration. He found solace and artistic inspiration in the picturesque

countryside, cypress trees, wheat fields, and blooming flowers.

3. "Starry Night": One of Van Gogh's most famous works, "Starry Night," was painted during his time in Saint-Rémy-de-Provence. The painting captures the view from his room at the asylum, showcasing a swirling sky, vibrant stars, and a sense of emotional intensity.

4. Asylum and Gardens: Visitors can explore the Saint-Paul-de-Mausole asylum, which still operates as a psychiatric institution. The gardens of the asylum, with their serene atmosphere and vibrant flora, offer a glimpse into the landscapes that inspired Van Gogh's artwork.

5. Musée Estrine: The Musée Estrine, located in the centre of Saint-Rémy-de-Provence, houses an extensive collection of Van Gogh's works. The museum showcases paintings, drawings, and personal correspondence that provide insights into Van Gogh's time in the region.

6. Van Gogh Walking Tour:
Saint-Rémy-de-Provence offers a Van Gogh
walking tour that takes visitors to significant sites
connected to the artist. This self-guided tour
allows visitors to follow in Van Gogh's footsteps,
exploring the landscapes that inspired his
masterpieces.

7. Glanum: Located just outside
Saint-Rémy-de-Provence, the ancient Roman city
of Glanum is another notable site associated with
Van Gogh. The artist found inspiration in the
ancient ruins and created sketches and drawings of
the archaeological site.

Visiting Saint-Rémy-de-Provence provides a
unique opportunity to immerse oneself in the
world of Van Gogh and experience the landscapes
and scenes that inspired his remarkable artwork.
The town's connection to Van Gogh, along with its
picturesque surroundings, museums, and cultural
heritage, makes it a must-visit destination for art
enthusiasts and those interested in exploring the
artistic legacy of Van Gogh in Provence.

The Palais des Papes: Avignon's Majestic Palace

The Palais des Papes (Palace of the Popes) in Avignon, Provence, is a majestic mediaeval fortress and one of the most significant historical sites in France. Here's a detailed yet concise overview of the Palais des Papes:

1. Historical Significance: The Palais des Papes was the residence of the popes during the 14th century when Avignon served as the centre of the Catholic Church. It was here that seven successive popes resided from 1309 to 1377, during a period known as the Avignon Papacy.

2. Architectural Marvel: The palace is an architectural masterpiece, blending elements of Gothic and Romanesque styles. It is the largest Gothic palace in the world, covering an area of over 15,000 square metres and consisting of two main buildings, the Palais Vieux (Old Palace) and the Palais Neuf (New Palace).

3. Grand Chambers and Halls: The Palais des Papes features grand chambers and halls that reflect the power and opulence of the mediaeval papacy. Notable spaces include the Great Audience Hall, the Consistory, the Grand Tinel (Banquet Hall), and the Pope's private apartments.

4. Frescoes and Decorations: The palace boasts impressive frescoes that adorn its walls and ceilings. These artworks depict religious and historical scenes, showcasing the artistic and cultural richness of the period. Some of the most renowned frescoes include those by Matteo Giovannetti and Simone Martini.

5. Ramparts and Towers: The Palais des Papes is fortified with massive ramparts and towers, providing both defensive capabilities and a commanding presence over the city. Visitors can explore the ramparts, offering panoramic views of Avignon and the surrounding countryside.

6. UNESCO World Heritage Site: The Palais des Papes, along with the historic centre of Avignon, has been designated as a UNESCO World Heritage

site since 1995. It is recognized for its architectural significance and its representation of the ecclesiastical and political influence of the papacy during the Avignon Papacy era.

7. Cultural Events and Exhibitions: The Palais des Papes serves as a venue for various cultural events, including art exhibitions, concerts, and theatre performances. These events enrich the experience of visitors, providing a glimpse into the vibrant cultural scene of Avignon.

Visiting the Palais des Papes offers a captivating journey into the mediaeval history and power of the Catholic Church. The grandeur of its architecture, the remarkable frescoes, and the rich historical context make it a must-visit destination for history enthusiasts, architecture lovers, and those seeking to immerse themselves in the intriguing legacy of the Avignon Papacy.

Château d'If: Island Fortress of Intrigue

The Château d'If is an island fortress located in the Frioul archipelago off the coast of Marseille, Provence. It is a captivating site with a rich history and an aura of intrigue. Here's a detailed yet concise overview of the Château d'If:

1. Historical Significance: Built in the 16th century, the Château d'If played a significant role in the defence of Marseille and the surrounding region. It served as a fortress guarding the entrance to the harbour and as a prison during different periods of its history.

2. The Count of Monte Cristo Connection: The Château d'If gained literary fame through Alexandre Dumas' novel, "The Count of Monte Cristo." The book depicts the protagonist, Edmond Dantès, being imprisoned in the fortress and his subsequent escape.

3. Island Location and Scenic Views: Situated on the island of If, the fortress offers breathtaking views of the Mediterranean Sea and the coastline. Its isolated location and rugged beauty add to the allure of the site.

4. Architectural Features: The Château d'If showcases a blend of architectural styles, including mediaeval military fortifications and Renaissance elements. Visitors can explore the fortress and its various structures, such as the keep, the towers, the chapel, and the prison cells.

5. Prison History: The Château d'If served as a state prison during its history. It housed numerous political and religious prisoners, including Protestants and opponents of the monarchy. The conditions within the prison were harsh, and escape attempts were rare due to the fortress's isolated location.

6. Museum and Exhibitions: Today, the Château d'If is open to the public and houses a museum that provides insights into the fortress's history, its role as a prison, and its literary connection to

"The Count of Monte Cristo." Visitors can learn about the lives of the prisoners and the significance of the fortress in the region.

7. Boat Excursions: Access to the Château d'If is by boat, usually departing from Marseille's Old Port. Boat excursions offer an opportunity to enjoy the scenic beauty of the Frioul archipelago, with stops at Château d'If and other islands in the group.

The Château d'If, with its intriguing history, literary associations, and stunning island setting, attracts visitors who are captivated by its tales of imprisonment, daring escapes, and the spirit of adventure. It is a unique and must-visit destination for history buffs, literature enthusiasts, and those seeking to experience the allure of Provence's island fortress.

Adventure Activities

Hiking and Trekking

Hiking and trekking in Provence, France, offer breathtaking landscapes, diverse terrain, and a rich cultural experience. Here's some detailed yet concise information about hiking and trekking in Provence:

1. Popular Hiking Routes: The GR 4 and GR 9 trails are two of the most renowned long-distance hiking routes in Provence. The GR 4 passes through the stunning Verdon Gorge, lavender fields of Plateau de Valensole, and the Luberon Regional Nature Park. The GR 9 covers the picturesque landscapes of the Mercantour National Park and the scenic coastline of the French Riviera.

2. Coastal Trails: The Calanques National Park near Marseille is famous for its rugged limestone cliffs and pristine turquoise waters. Hiking along the coastal paths here provides panoramic views of the Mediterranean Sea and access to secluded beaches.

3. Lavender Fields: The Plateau de Valensole is a must-visit for nature enthusiasts. From mid-June to mid-July, the lavender fields are in full bloom, creating a magical purple landscape. Numerous trails around Valensole allow hikers to immerse themselves in the beauty of Provence's iconic lavender.

4. Mont Ventoux: Standing at 1,912 metres, Mont Ventoux is a challenging trekking destination. Known as the "Giant of Provence," it offers panoramic views from its summit. The ascent can be demanding, but the reward is a stunning vista that stretches as far as the eye can see.

5. Gorges du Verdon: The Verdon Gorge is a natural marvel often referred to as the "Grand Canyon of Europe." It provides excellent hiking opportunities with trails along the rim and down into the gorge. Hikers can admire the turquoise Verdon River winding its way through towering cliffs.

6. Hilltop Villages: Provence is renowned for its picturesque hilltop villages, such as Gordes,

Roussillon, and Bonnieux. These villages offer a mix of cultural heritage, charming architecture, and stunning views. Hiking trails often connect these villages, allowing visitors to explore the region's history and enjoy its scenic beauty.

7. Practical Tips: When hiking or trekking in Provence, it's essential to wear appropriate footwear and carry sufficient water, especially during the warmer months. Check weather conditions beforehand and be aware of any trail restrictions or closures. It's also a good idea to bring a map or use a GPS device to navigate the trails effectively.

Whether you choose to explore the lavender fields, venture into the canyons, conquer mountain peaks, or wander through enchanting villages, hiking and trekking in Provence offer a remarkable blend of natural beauty and cultural discovery.

Cycling Routes: Explore Provence's Beauty

Cycling in Provence allows you to immerse yourself in the region's stunning landscapes, charming villages, and rich cultural heritage. Here's some detailed yet concise information about cycling routes in Provence:

1. Mont Ventoux: Mont Ventoux, famous for its challenging ascent, is a magnet for cycling enthusiasts. The climb to the summit is a bucket-list experience, offering breathtaking views and a sense of accomplishment. Several routes lead to the top, catering to different skill levels and preferences.

2. Luberon: The Luberon region is a cyclist's paradise, boasting picturesque villages, vineyards, and rolling hills. The Luberon Circuit is a popular choice, taking you through Gordes, Roussillon, and Bonnieux. The route offers a blend of natural beauty and cultural exploration, with

opportunities to visit mediaeval castles and enjoy local cuisine.

3. Vaucluse Plateau: The Vaucluse Plateau is a scenic area known for its lavender fields, vineyards, and olive groves. Cycling here allows you to soak up the region's tranquillity while pedalling through charming Provençal landscapes. The villages of Sault and Malaucène serve as excellent starting points for exploring the plateau.

4. Gorges du Verdon: The Verdon Gorge not only offers fantastic hiking but also thrilling cycling opportunities. The Route des Crêtes is a scenic road that winds along the edge of the gorge, providing breathtaking views of the turquoise river below. It's a challenging route with several climbs and descents, but the rewards are worth it.

5. Alpilles: The Alpilles mountain range is another delightful area for cycling in Provence. The Alpilles Circuit takes you through picturesque villages like Les Baux-de-Provence and Saint-Rémy-de-Provence. This route combines

natural beauty with cultural landmarks, including the famous Roman ruins of Glanum.

6. Camargue: For a unique cycling experience, head to the Camargue region, known for its vast wetlands, flamingos, and wild horses. The flat terrain and network of bike paths make it an ideal destination for leisurely rides. Explore the charming towns of Saintes-Maries-de-la-Mer and Aigues-Mortes while enjoying the region's rich biodiversity.

7. Practical Tips: Before setting off on a cycling adventure in Provence, ensure you have a well-maintained bike, proper safety gear, and repair tools. Stay hydrated and carry snacks, especially on longer rides. Familiarise yourself with local traffic rules and respect the environment and local communities.

Cycling in Provence offers a unique way to discover the region's beauty, from lavender-filled landscapes to mediaeval villages and stunning natural wonders. So hop on your bike, embrace the

Provençal charm, and enjoy the unforgettable journey through this captivating region.

Watersports and Beaches: Coastal Adventures

The coastal region of Provence in France offers a wide range of watersports and beautiful beaches, making it a paradise for beach lovers and water enthusiasts. Here's some detailed yet concise information about watersports and beaches in Provence:

1. Windsurfing and Kitesurfing: The Mistral winds that sweep through the Mediterranean make Provence an excellent destination for windsurfing and kitesurfing. The beaches of Almanarre and Hyères are particularly popular due to their consistent winds and favourable conditions for these adrenaline-pumping sports.

2. Sailing and Yachting: With its stunning coastline and numerous marinas, Provence provides ample

opportunities for sailing and yachting adventures. From Marseille to Saint-Tropez, you'll find sailing schools, charter services, and regattas catering to sailors of all levels. Explore the charming coastal towns and islands as you navigate the azure waters.

3. Scuba Diving and Snorkelling: The crystal-clear waters of the Mediterranean offer excellent visibility for scuba diving and snorkelling. The Calanques National Park near Marseille is a favourite spot, boasting underwater caves, vibrant marine life, and dramatic rock formations. The Îles d'Hyères and the underwater nature reserve of Port-Cros are also popular diving destinations.

4. Stand-Up Paddleboarding (SUP): SUP has gained popularity along the Provence coastline, thanks to its versatility and accessibility. Explore the pristine bays, coves, and lagoons while paddling on a SUP board. Many rental services and guided tours are available, allowing you to discover hidden gems along the coast.

5. Beaches: Provence is renowned for its stunning beaches, offering a mix of sandy stretches, hidden coves, and vibrant beach clubs. Some notable beaches include Plage de Pampelonne near Saint-Tropez, Plage du Prado in Marseille, and Plage de l'Estagnol in Hyères. These beaches provide amenities such as sun loungers, beach bars, and water sports rentals.

6. Kayaking and Canoeing: The coastal rivers and calmer sections of the Mediterranean are ideal for kayaking and canoeing. The Argens River near Saint-Aygulf and the Sorgue River near Isle-sur-la-Sorgue offer picturesque routes through scenic landscapes, including lush vegetation and charming villages.

7. Practical Tips: When engaging in watersports in Provence, ensure you have the necessary equipment, including safety gear. Check local weather conditions and respect any regulations or restrictions in place. It's also essential to be aware of currents and tides for safe and enjoyable experiences on the water.

From thrilling water activities to idyllic beach days, Provence's coastal region offers a wide range of opportunities for water enthusiasts. Whether you're seeking adventure or relaxation, you'll find plenty of options to enjoy the sparkling waters and coastal beauty of this enchanting part of France.

Golfing: Stunning Settings

Golfing in Provence provides a unique opportunity to enjoy the sport amidst breathtaking landscapes and picturesque settings. Here's some detailed yet concise information about golf courses and stunning settings for golfing in Provence:

1. Golf de Pont-Royal: Located near the village of Mallemort, Golf de Pont-Royal is a renowned course designed by Severiano Ballesteros. Surrounded by vineyards and olive groves, this 18-hole course offers panoramic views of the Luberon Mountains and provides a challenging yet enjoyable golfing experience.

2. Golf de Servanes: Situated in the heart of the Alpilles Regional Nature Park, Golf de Servanes offers a stunning setting surrounded by olive trees, cypresses, and rocky outcrops. The 18-hole course, designed by Trent Jones Jr., integrates beautifully with the natural landscape, providing a memorable golfing experience.

3. Golf de Barbaroux: Located in Brignoles, Golf de Barbaroux is nestled amidst a vast Provençal estate and vineyards. This 18-hole championship course, designed by Pete Dye, showcases rolling hills, mature oak trees, and picturesque lakes. Its natural beauty and challenging layout make it a favourite among golf enthusiasts.

4. Golf du Château de Taulane: Situated in the Var department, Golf du Château de Taulane offers a unique golfing experience in a historic setting. The course is surrounded by the dramatic scenery of the Gorges du Verdon and the Estérel Mountains. With its castle-like clubhouse and panoramic views, it provides an unforgettable golfing experience.

5. Golf de Sainte-Maxime: Overlooking the Gulf of Saint-Tropez, Golf de Sainte-Maxime is a scenic course offering stunning sea views and Mediterranean landscapes. The 18-hole course, designed by Don Harradine, combines challenging holes with coastal beauty, making it a popular choice for golfers seeking both sport and scenery.

6. Golf de Saumane: Located near the Luberon village of Saumane-de-Vaucluse, this golf course offers a unique blend of natural beauty and historical charm. Set against the backdrop of the Vaucluse Mountains and the Saumane Castle, the 18-hole course provides a serene and picturesque setting for golfers.

7. Practical Tips: When golfing in Provence, it's advisable to make reservations in advance, especially during peak seasons. Familiarise yourself with the specific course rules and etiquette. Additionally, many golf courses in Provence offer facilities such as driving ranges, practice areas, and golf academies for enthusiasts of all skill levels.

Golfing in Provence allows you to combine your love for the sport with the region's stunning landscapes and historic charm. Whether you prefer challenging championship courses or scenic coastal settings, Provence offers a range of options to suit every golfer's preferences, promising an unforgettable golfing experience.

Hot Air Ballooning: Soar Above Provence

Hot air ballooning in Provence offers a unique and breathtaking way to experience the region's beauty from above. Here's some detailed yet concise information about hot air ballooning in Provence:

1. Launch Sites: There are several launch sites across Provence, each offering a different perspective of the region's landscapes. Popular locations include the Luberon region, the countryside around Avignon, and the Verdon Gorge. Ballooning companies typically choose

launch sites based on weather conditions and the desired flight path.

2. Scenic Views: Soaring above Provence in a hot air balloon allows you to witness the region's stunning landscapes from a whole new perspective. Enjoy panoramic views of lavender fields, vineyards, rolling hills, picturesque villages, and even the Mediterranean coastline in the distance. The ever-changing scenery provides a magical experience.

3. Peaceful Flight: Hot air ballooning offers a tranquil and peaceful flight experience. As you gently float above the landscapes, you'll feel a sense of serenity and freedom. The absence of engine noise allows you to fully immerse yourself in the breathtaking views and appreciate the silence of the skies.

4. Sunrise and Sunset Flights: To capture the most enchanting moments, hot air balloon rides in Provence are often scheduled during sunrise or sunset. These times of day offer soft, golden lighting that enhances the beauty of the

landscapes below. It's a truly magical experience as the colours of the sky transform.

5. Group and Private Rides: Ballooning companies in Provence offer both group and private rides. Group rides allow you to share the experience with other passengers, making it a social and memorable adventure. Private rides offer a more intimate experience, perfect for couples or small groups who wish to enjoy a personalised and romantic flight.

6. Safety and Professionalism: Hot air ballooning companies in Provence prioritise safety and adhere to strict regulations. They employ experienced pilots who are knowledgeable about the region and skilled in operating the balloons. Before taking off, passengers receive safety instructions and an overview of the flight itinerary.

7. Weather Considerations: Hot air ballooning is weather-dependent, and flights are subject to favourable conditions. Ballooning companies closely monitor weather forecasts to ensure safe and enjoyable flights. In case of unfavourable

weather conditions, flights may be rescheduled or cancelled for the safety of passengers.

Hot air ballooning in Provence offers a once-in-a-lifetime experience, allowing you to soar above the region's stunning landscapes and capture breathtaking views. Whether you choose a sunrise or sunset flight, a group adventure, or a private ride, this serene and awe-inspiring activity promises to create unforgettable memories of your time in Provence.

Shopping and Souvenirs

Provençal Markets: Shopper's Paradise

Provençal markets are vibrant and bustling markets located in the region of Provence in southern France. They are known for their lively atmosphere, colourful displays, and a wide variety of products. Provençal markets offer a unique shopping experience and are considered a shopper's paradise for both locals and tourists. Here are some key features and highlights of Provençal markets:

1. Traditional Products: Provençal markets are renowned for their offering of traditional, locally produced goods. You can find an array of fresh fruits, vegetables, and herbs, many of which are grown locally in the fertile lands of Provence. The markets also feature artisanal products such as olive oil, honey, cheeses, wines, and various regional specialties.

2. Arts and Crafts: In addition to food products, Provençal markets often showcase a vibrant display of arts and crafts. Local artisans and craftsmen offer handmade pottery, textiles, ceramics, jewellery, and decorative items. These unique creations reflect the rich cultural heritage of the region.

3. Provencal Cuisine: The markets provide an excellent opportunity to explore and savour the flavours of Provencal cuisine. You can find stalls selling freshly baked bread, pastries, and a variety of traditional dishes like ratatouille, bouillabaisse, and socca. Don't miss the chance to taste regional delicacies like lavender-infused products, nougat, and Calissons d'Aix.

4. Atmosphere and Ambiance: Provençal markets are known for their lively and convivial atmosphere. The markets are often set up in picturesque town squares, lined with colourful stalls, bustling with locals, and filled with the aromas of fresh produce and spices. The vendors

are friendly and enthusiastic, making the shopping experience even more enjoyable.

5. Seasonal Offerings: The markets change with the seasons, adapting to the availability of local produce. Spring and summer bring an abundance of vibrant fruits, vegetables, and flowers, while autumn showcases the harvest of grapes, olives, and chestnuts. Winter markets feature holiday specialties, including Christmas decorations and seasonal treats.

6. Weekly Market Schedule: Each town and village in Provence has its own designated market day(s). These markets typically take place once or twice a week, although some larger towns may have more frequent markets. It is advisable to check the specific market schedules of the places you plan to visit.

7. Cultural Experience: Beyond shopping, Provençal markets offer a glimpse into the region's cultural heritage. They are an integral part of local life, and visiting the markets provides an opportunity to interact with locals, learn about

their traditions, and immerse yourself in the Provençal way of life.

Overall, Provençal markets are a shopper's paradise, offering a wide range of traditional products, regional delicacies, and unique crafts. Whether you are looking to explore the local cuisine, purchase artisanal goods, or simply soak up the vibrant ambiance, a visit to these markets is an essential part of experiencing the charm and authenticity of Provence.

Artisanal Crafts and Local Products

Provence in southern France is known for its rich tradition of artisanal crafts and locally produced goods. Here is some detailed yet concise information on artisanal crafts and local products you can find in Provence:

1. Pottery and Ceramics: Provence is famous for its exquisite pottery and ceramics. Artisans create

beautifully hand-painted plates, bowls, vases, and tiles, often featuring vibrant colours and traditional patterns inspired by the region's nature and culture.

2. Textiles: The region is renowned for its high-quality fabrics and textiles. Local artisans weave and dye fabrics to create Provençal-style tablecloths, napkins, towels, and clothing. The fabrics often showcase bright colours, intricate patterns, and motifs inspired by nature and local traditions.

3. Soap and Perfumes: Provence is home to the famous Marseille soap, a traditional soap made from natural vegetable oils. Many towns in the region have soap factories and artisanal soap makers, offering a variety of scented and decorative soaps. Perfumeries in Grasse, the perfume capital of the world, produce exquisite fragrances using local flowers and herbs like lavender, rose, and jasmine.

4. Olive Oil: Provence is known for its high-quality olive oil production. The region's sunny climate

and fertile soil contribute to the cultivation of olives, resulting in a range of flavorful and aromatic oils. You can find artisanal olive oil producers offering different varieties and blends at markets and local shops.

5. Honey and Bee Products: The diverse flora of Provence provides an ideal environment for beekeeping. Local beekeepers produce delicious and fragrant honey, often infused with flavours like lavender or thyme. Additionally, you can find other bee products such as beeswax candles and cosmetics made with honey and beeswax.

6. Herbs and Spices: The sunny hills of Provence are known for their aromatic herbs and spices. Local markets offer a variety of dried herbs like thyme, rosemary, and savoury, as well as blends like Herbes de Provence. These flavorful ingredients are essential for traditional Provençal cuisine.

7. Regional Specialties: Provence boasts a wide range of unique regional specialties. These include traditional candies like Calissons d'Aix, nougat,

and candied fruits. Other local treats include lavender-infused products such as honey, chocolates, and essential oils.

8. Wines: Provence is renowned for its wine production. The region is known for its rosé wines, which benefit from the Mediterranean climate and vineyards that stretch across picturesque landscapes. Visiting local wineries and vineyards allows you to sample and purchase a variety of wines directly from the source.

Exploring artisanal crafts and local products in Provence provides an opportunity to appreciate the region's rich cultural heritage and support local artisans and producers. Whether it's bringing home a piece of hand-painted pottery, indulging in fragrant soaps and perfumes, or savouring the flavours of local honey, olive oil, and wine, these products serve as tangible reminders of the beauty and authenticity of Provence.

Antique Hunting in Provence

Antique hunting in Provence offers a delightful adventure for enthusiasts seeking unique and historic treasures. Here is some detailed yet concise information on antique hunting in Provence:

1. Antique Markets: Provence is home to numerous antique markets, where you can explore a vast array of vintage and antique items. Popular markets include the L'Isle-sur-la-Sorgue Sunday Market, which is renowned for its antique dealers and picturesque setting along the canals. Other notable markets include the Villeneuve-lès-Avignon Antique Market and the Aix-en-Provence Antique Fair.

2. Brocantes: Brocantes are flea markets or second-hand markets that offer a mix of antique, vintage, and used items. These markets can be found throughout Provence, often in smaller towns and villages. Brocantes are excellent places to uncover hidden gems, from furniture and home

decor to clothing and collectibles. The ambiance is often lively, and bargaining is expected.

3. Antique Shops and Galleries: Provence is dotted with antique shops and galleries, where you can explore carefully curated collections of antique furniture, art, jewellery, and decorative items. Towns like Avignon, Arles, and Marseille have a concentration of such establishments, each with its own unique selection and atmosphere. These shops offer a more refined and curated antique shopping experience.

4. Village Garage Sales: Some villages in Provence hold annual or seasonal garage sales, where locals set up stalls to sell their unwanted items. These garage sales can be a treasure trove for antique hunters, as you may stumble upon unexpected finds at affordable prices. Keep an eye out for signs advertising "vide-greniers" or "brocante" sales in the area.

5. Antique Fairs and Events: Provence hosts various antique fairs and events throughout the year, attracting collectors and dealers from near

and far. These events showcase a wide range of antiques, including furniture, artwork, ceramics, textiles, and more. The Foire Internationale d'Antiquités et Brocante in L'Isle-sur-la-Sorgue is a prominent annual antique fair that draws antique lovers from around the world.

6. Authentic Provencal Pieces: Antique hunting in Provence offers an opportunity to acquire authentic Provencal pieces that reflect the region's rich history and craftsmanship. Look for items like Provençal furniture, traditional pottery, vintage textiles with regional motifs, and antique religious artefacts. These pieces can add a touch of charm and history to your home or collection.

7. Expertise and Authenticity: When antique hunting in Provence, it's important to exercise caution and seek out reputable sellers. If you are searching for valuable or rare items, consider consulting with local experts or appraisers to ensure the authenticity and value of your finds.

Antique hunting in Provence combines the thrill of discovery with the charm of the region's history and craftsmanship. Whether you explore bustling antique markets, peruse quaint village shops, or attend specialised fairs, you are sure to find unique treasures that add character and beauty to your collection.

Fashion and Design: Provence's Style

Fashion and design in Provence embrace a distinctive style that reflects the region's natural beauty, rich history, and relaxed Mediterranean lifestyle. Here is some detailed yet concise information on Provence's fashion and design:

1. Provençal Prints and Fabrics: Provence is renowned for its vibrant and colourful prints that adorn fabrics used in fashion and home decor. The iconic Provençal prints feature floral motifs, such as lavender, sunflowers, and olives, as well as traditional patterns like paisley and toile de Jouy. These prints are often seen on dresses, skirts,

shirts, and accessories, creating a cheerful and summery aesthetic.

2. Natural and Light Fabrics: Given the region's warm climate, fashion in Provence emphasises the use of natural and breathable fabrics. Cotton, linen, and silk are popular choices, as they provide comfort and allow for airflow. These fabrics are used in a variety of clothing items, from flowing dresses and lightweight blouses to loose-fitting pants and skirts.

3. Pastel Colours: The colour palette of Provence's fashion and design tends to be soft and pastel, inspired by the region's landscape and the delicate hues of its flowers and countryside. Shades like lavender, pale yellow, soft pink, and sky blue are commonly found in clothing, accessories, and home decor.

4. Effortless and Relaxed Silhouettes: The fashion style in Provence leans towards effortless and relaxed silhouettes that capture the laid-back Mediterranean lifestyle. Loose-fitting dresses, airy tops, and wide-leg pants are popular choices,

allowing for ease of movement and comfort. Flowing lines and breezy cuts are characteristic of Provençal fashion.

5. Straw Accessories: Straw accessories are synonymous with Provence's fashion, adding a touch of rustic charm to the overall look. Straw hats, woven baskets, and woven handbags are popular choices and are often adorned with ribbons, flowers, or embroidered details.

6. Traditional Provençal Costumes: The traditional costumes of Provence, known as "costumes d'Arles," continue to inspire contemporary fashion and design. These costumes feature intricate embroidery, lace, and decorative elements, representing the rich cultural heritage of the region. Some fashion designers incorporate elements of these traditional costumes into modern designs, paying homage to Provence's history.

7. Local Artisans and Designers: Provence is home to a vibrant community of artisans and designers who create unique fashion pieces and accessories.

Local artisans often draw inspiration from the region's natural surroundings, traditional crafts, and cultural heritage. Exploring boutique shops and markets allows you to discover one-of-a-kind creations and support local talent.

Provence's fashion and design reflect a blend of rustic charm, relaxed elegance, and a touch of whimsy. From the vibrant Provençal prints and pastel colours to the use of natural fabrics and effortless silhouettes, the style of Provence captures the essence of the region's enchanting landscapes and laid-back lifestyle.

Festivals and Events

Aix-en-Provence Festival: Cultural Extravaganza

The Aix-en-Provence Festival is a renowned cultural event that takes place annually in the city of Aix-en-Provence, located in the Provence region of southern France. It is known for its grandeur, artistic excellence, and diverse program offerings, attracting both local and international visitors.

Here are some key details about the Aix-en-Provence Festival:

1. History: The festival was founded in 1948 by Gabriel Dussurget, an opera lover and visionary, with the aim of revitalising the operatic tradition in Aix-en-Provence. Since then, it has grown into one of the most prestigious and influential cultural festivals in Europe.

2. Duration: The festival usually takes place during the months of June and July, spanning several weeks. It offers a rich and varied program that includes opera, classical music concerts, recitals, dance performances, and theatrical productions.

3. Venues: Performances are held at various historic and picturesque locations throughout Aix-en-Provence, including the magnificent Théâtre de l'Archevêché, which serves as the festival's main venue. Other notable venues include the Grand Théâtre de Provence and the Hôtel Maynier d'Oppède.

4. Artistic Excellence: The festival is known for its commitment to artistic excellence, showcasing world-class performers, renowned orchestras, acclaimed opera companies, and distinguished conductors and directors. It has hosted some of the most influential figures in the performing arts, including Leonard Bernstein, Herbert von Karajan, and Peter Brook.

5. Opera: Opera plays a central role in the Aix-en-Provence Festival. It presents a diverse

repertoire, ranging from classic works by composers such as Mozart, Verdi, and Puccini to contemporary and lesser-known pieces. The festival often commissions and premieres new operatic works, contributing to the development of the art form.

6. Contemporary Focus: In addition to opera, the festival has a strong emphasis on contemporary and innovative productions. It regularly collaborates with leading contemporary composers, directors, and artists, promoting experimentation and pushing the boundaries of traditional performance.

7. Cultural Engagement: The Aix-en-Provence Festival actively engages with the local community and promotes cultural exchange. It organises educational programs, workshops, and masterclasses for aspiring artists and provides opportunities for emerging talents. It also fosters collaborations with international cultural institutions and hosts artists from around the world.

8. Provencal Charm: The festival's location in the picturesque city of Aix-en-Provence adds to its allure. Known for its charming streets, vibrant cultural scene, and rich historical heritage, Aix-en-Provence offers a delightful backdrop for festival attendees to immerse themselves in the arts and explore the beauty of the region.

The Aix-en-Provence Festival is a cultural extravaganza that celebrates the performing arts in all their forms. With its rich history, commitment to artistic excellence, and stunning setting, it continues to enchant audiences and inspire artists from across the globe.

Fête de la Lavande: Lavender in the Spotlight

Fête de la Lavande, also known as the Lavender Festival, is a delightful celebration that showcases the vibrant beauty and cultural significance of lavender in the Provence region of southern France. It offers visitors a unique opportunity to immerse themselves in the world of lavender through various events and activities.

Here are some key details about Fête de la Lavande:

1. Lavender in Provence: Provence is renowned for its sprawling lavender fields that blanket the countryside with hues of purple and release a fragrant aroma. Lavender has been cultivated in the region for centuries and holds a special place in Provencal culture and traditions.

2. Celebration of Lavender: Fête de la Lavande serves as a grand celebration of this iconic flower. It usually takes place during the summer months, typically in July when lavender is in full bloom, and attracts both locals and tourists.

3. Location: The festival is held in different locations throughout Provence, particularly in villages and towns known for their lavender production. Popular locations include Valensole, Sault, and Digne-les-Bains.

4. Lavender Fields: One of the highlights of the festival is the opportunity to explore the magnificent lavender fields. Visitors can wander through the blooming fields, capturing stunning photographs and enjoying the sensory experience of the lavender's soothing scent and vibrant colours.

5. Festive Atmosphere: Fête de la Lavande is a lively and colourful event with a festive atmosphere. It features various activities such as parades, street performances, live music, traditional dances, and local artisans showcasing lavender-based products.

6. Lavender Products: The festival provides an excellent platform for local producers and artisans to display and sell their lavender-based products. Visitors can find a wide range of lavender-infused items, including essential oils, soaps, perfumes, candles, culinary products, and handmade crafts.

7. Workshops and Demonstrations: Fête de la Lavande offers workshops and demonstrations where attendees can learn about lavender

cultivation, harvesting techniques, and traditional lavender-related crafts. These interactive sessions provide insights into the rich cultural heritage associated with lavender.

8. Culinary Delights: Lavender is not only appreciated for its beauty and fragrance but also for its culinary uses. During the festival, visitors can sample and savour a variety of lavender-infused culinary delights, such as lavender honey, lavender ice cream, lavender-infused drinks, and lavender-flavoured pastries.

9. Cultural Traditions: The Lavender Festival also showcases the cultural traditions and folklore of the region. Traditional costumes, folk dances, and music performances add a touch of authenticity and allow visitors to delve into the local heritage.

Fête de la Lavande is a captivating celebration that pays homage to the enchanting lavender fields of Provence. Through its festivities, visitors can indulge in the beauty, scents, and flavours of lavender while immersing themselves in the cultural traditions of the region.

Nice Carnival: Colourful Spectacle

The Nice Carnival is a vibrant and spectacular event held annually in the city of Nice, located in the Provence-Alpes-Côte d'Azur region of southern France. Known for its colourful parades, elaborate floats, and festive atmosphere, it is one of the most renowned carnivals in the world.

Here are some key details about the Nice Carnival:

1. History and Tradition: The Nice Carnival has a rich history dating back to the 13th century, making it one of the oldest carnivals in Europe. It is deeply rooted in the local culture and has evolved over the centuries, blending traditional customs with modern artistic expressions.

2. Duration: The carnival usually takes place over a period of two weeks, starting in late February and extending into early March. The festivities include both daytime and nighttime events, with the highlight being the colourful parades that wind through the streets of Nice.

3. Theme and Floats: Each year, the carnival adopts a specific theme that sets the tone for the festivities. Elaborate floats, adorned with intricate decorations and imaginative designs, take centre stage during the parades. These floats, often several metres tall, are meticulously crafted and showcase the creativity and craftsmanship of the carnival organisers.

4. Parade Processions: The parades feature a mix of professional artists, local performers, musicians, and costumed participants who entertain the crowd with lively dances, acrobatics, and theatrical displays. Colourful confetti, streamers, and bursts of music add to the festive ambiance.

5. Flower Battles: A unique highlight of the Nice Carnival is the "Bataille de Fleurs" or Flower Battle. During this event, elaborately decorated floats adorned with fresh flowers move through the streets, while participants on the floats throw flowers into the crowd. It creates a captivating scene of floral beauty and joyful interaction between the participants and spectators.

6. Nighttime Parades: In addition to the daytime parades, the Nice Carnival offers nighttime parades known as "Corsos Illuminés." These parades feature illuminated floats, adorned with vibrant lights and stunning visual effects, creating a magical atmosphere as they pass through the streets.

7. Masked Revellers: The carnival encourages attendees to participate in the festivities by donning masks and costumes. Visitors can join in the revelry by dressing up in elaborate disguises, adding to the colourful and whimsical atmosphere of the event.

8. Cultural and Artistic Performances: The Nice Carnival showcases a diverse range of cultural and artistic performances, including music concerts, dance shows, street theatre, and fireworks displays. These events take place in various locations throughout Nice, adding to the carnival's overall spectacle.

9. Local Traditions: The carnival embraces the traditions and customs of the region, including the use of traditional Provençal music and dance forms. Visitors can experience the unique blend of local culture and carnival traditions, creating a truly immersive and memorable experience.

The Nice Carnival is a dazzling and joyful celebration that captivates both locals and visitors alike. With its elaborate floats, lively parades, and festive spirit, it offers a colourful spectacle that showcases the creativity, artistry, and cultural heritage of the Provence region.

Avignon Theatre Festival: Celebrating Performing Arts

The Avignon Theatre Festival is a prominent event that celebrates the performing arts in the city of Avignon, located in the Provence region of southern France. Renowned for its rich theatrical tradition, the festival brings together a diverse range of performances and artists from around the world.

Here are some key details about the Avignon Theatre Festival:

1. History and Significance: The festival was established in 1947 by Jean Vilar, a visionary theatre director. It played a crucial role in revitalising theatre in France and promoting innovative and thought-provoking performances. Today, it is one of the most prestigious theatre festivals in the world.

2. Duration and Schedule: The Avignon Theatre Festival typically takes place in July and lasts for

several weeks. It features an extensive program of theatre, dance, music, and other performing arts, showcasing a wide range of genres and styles.

3. Venues: Performances are held in various venues throughout Avignon, including historic theatres, churches, outdoor spaces, and unconventional locations. The most famous venue is the Palais des Papes (Palace of the Popes), a UNESCO World Heritage site, which provides a stunning backdrop for theatrical productions.

4. International Participation: The festival attracts artists and theatre companies from around the globe, offering a platform for cross-cultural exchange and artistic collaboration. It serves as a meeting point for theatre professionals, critics, and enthusiasts, fostering dialogue and exploration of new ideas.

5. Official Selection: The festival has an official selection process, curated by a team of experts who carefully choose a diverse and compelling lineup of performances. These selections often

reflect contemporary social and political themes, and include both established and emerging artists.

6. Main Program and Off Festival: The Avignon Theatre Festival is divided into two main components. The "In" program comprises major productions that are selected for official presentation. Additionally, the "Off" festival features a vibrant fringe program, with independent and alternative theatre companies staging performances throughout the city.

7. Avignon OFF: The Off festival is an integral part of the Avignon Theatre Festival and has gained its own recognition and following over the years. It offers a platform for emerging artists, experimental works, and innovative theatre forms. The Off program spans a wide range of genres, from classic plays to contemporary performances and avant-garde productions.

8. Street Performances and Events: Avignon transforms into a bustling hub of artistic energy during the festival, with street performances, open-air events, and artistic installations taking

place throughout the city. The streets come alive with impromptu performances, creating a vibrant and immersive atmosphere for both locals and visitors.

9. Cultural Impact: The Avignon Theatre Festival has had a significant impact on the cultural landscape of Avignon and France as a whole. It has contributed to the city's reputation as a theatre capital and continues to inspire artistic expression, innovation, and dialogue within the performing arts community.

The Avignon Theatre Festival is a celebration of creativity, artistic excellence, and cultural exchange. With its diverse program, international participation, and dynamic atmosphere, it offers an immersive and enriching experience for theatre lovers and artists alike, making it a highlight of the performing arts scene in Provence.

Les Rencontres d'Arles: Photography at Its Finest

Les Rencontres d'Arles, also known as the Arles Photography Festival, is a prestigious event that showcases photography at its finest in the city of Arles, located in the Provence region of southern France. It is one of the most important photography festivals in the world, attracting photographers, artists, and photography enthusiasts from around the globe.

Here are some key details about Les Rencontres d'Arles:

1. History and Significance: The festival was founded in 1970 by photographer Lucien Clergue, writer Michel Tournier, and historian Jean-Maurice Rouquette. It was created to promote and celebrate photography as an art form and has since become a significant platform for emerging talents as well as established photographers.

2. Duration and Schedule: Les Rencontres d'Arles typically takes place from July to September, spanning several months. The festival presents a diverse and extensive program of exhibitions, workshops, screenings, and discussions, attracting a wide audience of photography enthusiasts and professionals.

3. Exhibition Spaces: The festival utilises various historic and contemporary exhibition spaces throughout Arles, including former industrial buildings, churches, galleries, and public spaces. These venues provide unique settings for the display of photographic works, creating an immersive experience for visitors.

4. International Selection: The festival features a curated selection of exhibitions that showcase the work of renowned photographers from around the world. The program includes both solo and group exhibitions, covering a wide range of genres and themes within the realm of photography.

5. Emerging Talent: Les Rencontres d'Arles is known for its commitment to supporting emerging

photographers and promoting their work. It provides a platform for young and upcoming artists to showcase their talent alongside established names, fostering creativity and innovation within the field of photography.

6. Special Projects and Installations: In addition to traditional exhibitions, the festival often features special projects and installations that push the boundaries of photography as an art form. These projects explore experimental techniques, multimedia presentations, and interactive experiences, offering a fresh perspective on the medium.

7. Awards and Recognition: Les Rencontres d'Arles awards several prizes to photographers and artists whose work stands out during the festival. These awards, including the prestigious Discovery Award and the Author Book Award, contribute to the recognition and promotion of exceptional talent within the field of photography.

8. Educational Programs: The festival organises a series of educational programs, workshops, and

portfolio reviews for aspiring photographers, providing opportunities for learning, skill development, and networking. These initiatives support the growth and development of emerging talents and contribute to the overall enrichment of the photography community.

9. Arles as a Cultural Hub: The city of Arles itself adds to the charm and appeal of the festival. With its rich historical heritage, including the Roman amphitheatre and other architectural marvels, Arles provides a captivating backdrop for the celebration of photography and offers a unique cultural experience for festival attendees.

Les Rencontres d'Arles is a celebration of photography as an art form, bringing together established and emerging talents in a vibrant and dynamic festival. With its diverse exhibitions, special projects, and educational initiatives, it continues to shape the photography landscape and inspire artists and enthusiasts in Provence and beyond.

Practical Information and Tips

Language and Local Customs

Provence is a region in southeastern France known for its rich cultural heritage and vibrant local customs. Here's some detailed yet concise information about the language and local customs in Provence:

1. Language: The primary language spoken in Provence is French. However, due to its unique history and geographic location, the region also has a distinctive dialect known as Provençal or Occitan. Provençal has deep roots in the region and is still spoken by a small number of people, particularly in rural areas. Nevertheless, French is widely understood and used for official purposes, commerce, and everyday communication.

2. Local Customs: Provence has a rich cultural tapestry shaped by its history, Mediterranean

climate, and proximity to the sea. Some notable local customs include:

a. Cuisine: Provence is renowned for its delicious Mediterranean cuisine, which features fresh ingredients like olive oil, herbs (such as thyme, rosemary, and basil), garlic, tomatoes, and seafood. Dishes like bouillabaisse (fish stew), ratatouille (vegetable stew), and pissaladière (onion and anchovy tart) are popular in the region.

b. Markets: Traditional open-air markets, known as "marchés," are an integral part of Provençal life. These markets are bustling with locals and visitors who come to purchase fresh produce, regional specialties, handicrafts, and clothing. The markets offer a vibrant and colourful experience, where bargaining and sampling local delicacies are common practices.

c. Festivals: Provence is known for its lively festivals that celebrate various aspects of local culture and tradition. One of the most famous festivals is the Feria d'Arles, which takes place in Arles and showcases traditional bullfighting, parades, music, and dancing. Other notable festivals include the Fête de la Saint-Jean (Midsummer Festival), lavender festivals, and grape harvest celebrations.

d. Traditional Clothing: Although modern clothing styles are prevalent, you can still find people in Provence wearing traditional attire on special occasions or during festivals. The costumes often feature regional variations, with women wearing long, colourful skirts, embroidered blouses, and straw hats, while men may don a wide-brimmed hat called a "chapeau de paille" and a loose-fitting shirt.

e. Folklore and Traditions: Provence has a rich folklore tradition with mythical characters like the "santons" (hand-painted nativity scene figurines), the "lou ravi" (the fool), and legends associated with the Camargue region. Traditional Provençal games, such as pétanque (a form of boules), also play a significant role in local culture.

Overall, Provence's language and local customs reflect the region's distinct identity, blending

French influences with its unique Provençal heritage. From its vibrant cuisine and bustling markets to its colourful festivals and traditional clothing, Provence offers a captivating cultural experience.

Safety and Emergency Contacts

Safety is an important aspect to consider when travelling to any destination. Here's some detailed yet concise information about safety and emergency contacts in Provence:

1. General Safety: Provence is generally considered a safe destination for travellers. However, it's always advisable to take common safety precautions, such as:

   a. Secure your belongings: Keep an eye on your personal belongings and avoid displaying valuable items in public. Use hotel safes or secure lockers for passports, cash, and other important documents.

b. Stay informed: Stay updated on local news, weather conditions, and any travel advisories or warnings issued by your country's embassy or consulate.

c. Be cautious in crowded areas: Exercise caution in crowded tourist areas, as petty theft can occur. Keep your belongings secure and be aware of your surroundings.

d. Road safety: If you plan to drive in Provence, familiarise yourself with local traffic laws and be cautious on narrow or winding roads. Avoid excessive speeding and drink driving.

2. Emergency Contacts:

a. Emergency services: In case of a life-threatening emergency, dial the European emergency number 112 to reach police, ambulance, or fire services. This number is valid across all European Union member states, including France.

b. Police: If you need to contact the police for non-emergency situations or to report a crime, dial 17.

c. Medical emergencies: In case of a medical emergency, dial 15 to reach the emergency medical services (SAMU) for immediate assistance.

d. Tourist helpline: The Provence-Alpes-Côte d'Azur region has a tourist helpline that provides information and assistance to travellers. You can contact them at +33 (0)892 680 222 (€0.34 per minute) for general inquiries and tourist-related assistance.

e. Embassy or consulate: If you're a foreign traveller and require assistance from your country's embassy or consulate, locate their contact information before your trip and keep it handy. They can provide support in case of emergencies or other unforeseen circumstances.

It's important to note that emergency contact numbers and services may vary slightly, so it's always a good idea to check for the most up-to-date information before your trip. Additionally, having travel insurance that covers medical emergencies and trip cancellation can provide added peace of mind during your visit to Provence.

Health and Medical Services

When it comes to health and medical services, Provence offers a reliable and well-developed healthcare system. Here's some detailed yet concise information about health and medical services in Provence:

1. Healthcare System: France has a high standard of healthcare, and Provence benefits from this comprehensive system. Both public and private medical facilities are available throughout the region, including hospitals, clinics, and specialised medical centres.

2. Emergency Medical Services: In case of a medical emergency, dial the European emergency number 112 to reach emergency services. This

number will connect you to the appropriate medical assistance, including ambulance services.

3. Health Insurance: It's important to have adequate health insurance coverage when visiting Provence. If you are a European Union citizen, carrying a valid European Health Insurance Card (EHIC) will ensure that you can access necessary healthcare services on the same terms as the local population. Non-EU visitors should obtain comprehensive travel insurance that includes medical coverage.

4. Pharmacies: Pharmacies, known as "pharmacies" or "pharmacies de garde," can be found in towns and cities across Provence. They are easily recognizable by a green cross sign. Pharmacies are well-stocked and can provide over-the-counter medications, prescription medications, and basic medical advice. Some pharmacies operate on a rotational basis to ensure that there is always one open during evenings, weekends, and holidays.

5. Language: The primary language spoken by healthcare professionals in Provence is French. However, many medical staff, particularly in popular tourist areas, can communicate in English. It's helpful to carry a basic medical phrasebook or translation app to facilitate communication if necessary.

6. Travel Vaccinations: Before travelling to Provence, it's advisable to check if any specific vaccinations are recommended or required. Consult your local healthcare provider or travel clinic to ensure that you are up to date on routine vaccinations and to discuss any additional vaccines that may be recommended based on your individual health and travel plans.

7. Travel Medications: If you require prescription medications, ensure you bring an adequate supply for the duration of your stay in Provence. It's also a good idea to carry a copy of your prescriptions, as well as a letter from your healthcare provider explaining the medical condition and the necessity of the prescribed medications.

8. Health and Safety Precautions: Provence generally has good health and hygiene standards. It's important to take common health precautions such as practising good hand hygiene, drinking bottled water or using a water filter, and consuming food from reputable establishments.

Remember, this information is a general overview, and it's recommended to consult with your healthcare provider or travel clinic before your trip to obtain personalised advice based on your specific needs and medical history.

Packing Essentials

When packing for a trip to Provence, it's important to consider the region's climate, activities, and cultural norms. Here's some detailed yet concise information on packing essentials for your trip to Provence:

1. Clothing:
  – Lightweight and breathable clothing: Provence has a Mediterranean climate with hot summers, so

pack lightweight and breathable clothes like cotton shirts, dresses, shorts, and skirts.

- Sun protection: Don't forget to pack a wide-brimmed hat, sunglasses, and sunscreen to protect yourself from the sun's rays.

- Comfortable walking shoes: Bring comfortable shoes for exploring the picturesque towns, villages, and countryside. Consider closed-toe shoes for uneven terrain and hiking sandals for outdoor activities.

- Layering options: Although summers are hot, evenings can be cooler, especially in spring and autumn. Pack a light jacket or sweater for layering.

2. Accessories:

- Daypack or tote bag: A small daypack or tote bag is useful for carrying essentials, such as a water bottle, sunscreen, snacks, and a guidebook, during your day trips.

- Scarf or shawl: A lightweight scarf or shawl can be handy for covering your shoulders when visiting religious sites or providing additional warmth during cooler evenings.

- Swimwear: If you plan to enjoy the beautiful Mediterranean beaches or hotel pools, pack swimwear.

3. Practical Items:

- Travel adapter: France uses Type E electrical outlets, so bring a travel adapter to charge your electronic devices.

- Portable charger: Keep a portable charger handy for recharging your smartphone or other devices while on the go.

- Travel documents: Carry a copy of your passport, travel insurance, and any other important documents. It's also advisable to have digital copies stored securely in the cloud or email.

4. Miscellaneous:

- Medications: If you take prescription medications, ensure you have an adequate supply for the duration of your trip. It's also a good idea to carry a small first-aid kit with essentials like band-aids, pain relievers, and any necessary personal medications.

- Travel guidebook or map: While digital resources are readily available, having a physical travel guidebook or map can be helpful for exploring the region, finding local recommendations, and navigating smaller towns and villages.

5. Respectful Attire:
   - Modest clothing: When visiting religious sites or participating in cultural events, it's respectful to dress modestly. Carry a lightweight cardigan or scarf to cover bare shoulders if needed.

Remember to check the weather forecast before your trip to ensure you pack accordingly. Additionally, consider any specific activities you plan to engage in, such as hiking or visiting upscale restaurants, and pack accordingly. By packing these essentials, you'll be well-prepared to enjoy the beauty and charm of Provence while staying comfortable and respectful.

Useful Phrases and Basic French Vocabulary

When travelling to Provence, having some basic French vocabulary and useful phrases can greatly enhance your experience. Here's some detailed yet concise information on useful phrases and basic French vocabulary to help you communicate effectively:

1. Greetings and Basic Phrases:
   - Hello: Bonjour (bohn-zhoor)
   - Goodbye: Au revoir (oh ruh-vwahr)
   - Please: S'il vous plaît (seel voo pleh)
   - Thank you: Merci (mehr-see)
   - Yes: Oui (wee)
   - No: Non (nohn)
   - Excuse me: Excusez-moi (ehks-kyoo-zay mwa)
   - Sorry: Pardon (par-dohn)
   - I don't understand: Je ne comprends pas (zhuh nuh kohm-prahn pah)
   - Do you speak English?: Parlez-vous anglais ? (par-lay voo ahn-glay)

2. Ordering Food and Drinks:

   - I would like...: Je voudrais... (zhuh voo-dreh)

   - Menu: Menu (meh-noo)

   - Water: Eau (oh)

   - Coffee: Café (ka-fay)

   - Wine: Vin (van)

   - Beer: Bière (byehr)

   - Can I have the bill, please?: L'addition, s'il vous plaît (lah-dee-syohn, seel voo pleh)

3. Directions and Transportation:

   - Where is...?: Où est...? (oo ay)

   - Train station: Gare (gahr)

   - Bus stop: Arrêt de bus (ah-ray duh boos)

   - Left: À gauche (ah gohsh)

   - Right: À droite (ah drwaht)

   - Straight ahead: Tout droit (too drwah)

4. Shopping and Sightseeing:

   - How much is it?: Combien ça coûte ? (kohm-byahn sah koot)

   - I'm just looking: Je regarde seulement (zhuh ruh-gahrd suh-luh-mahn)

- Where is the restroom?: Où sont les toilettes ?
(oo sohn lay twah-leht)

5. Emergency Situations:
   - Help!: Au secours ! (oh suh-koor)
   - I need a doctor: J'ai besoin d'un médecin (zhay
buh-zwahn duhn meh-deh-sahn)
   - Call the police: Appelez la police (ah-peh-lay
lah poh-lees)

Remember, attempting to speak a few basic
phrases in French shows respect and can make
interactions more pleasant. The locals appreciate
the effort, even if your pronunciation isn't perfect.
Carry a pocket-sized phrasebook or use translation
apps for additional assistance when needed. Enjoy
your time in Provence!

Day Trips

Cassis: Azure Waters and Cliffside Charm

Cassis is a picturesque coastal town located in the Provence-Alpes-Côte d'Azur region of southern France. It is known for its azure waters, towering cliffs, and charming atmosphere. Here is some detailed and short information about Cassis:

Location: Cassis is situated on the Mediterranean coast, about 20 kilometres east of Marseille. It is nestled between the Calanques National Park and the Cap Canaille, which is the highest sea cliff in France.

Scenic Beauty: One of the main attractions of Cassis is its stunning natural beauty. The town is surrounded by dramatic limestone cliffs that plunge into the clear turquoise waters of the Mediterranean Sea. The combination of the azure sea, white cliffs, and lush greenery creates a breathtaking landscape.

Calanques: Cassis is renowned for its calanques, which are narrow and steep-walled inlets carved into the cliffs. These natural formations are a paradise for nature lovers and outdoor enthusiasts. Visitors can explore the calanques by boat, kayak, or by hiking along the well-marked trails.

Beaches: Cassis offers several beautiful beaches where visitors can relax and enjoy the sun. The most popular beach is Plage de la Grande Mer, located near the town centre. It features golden sand and calm waters, ideal for swimming and sunbathing.

Port and Village: The picturesque harbour of Cassis is lined with colourful fishing boats and vibrant waterfront cafes. Strolling along the port, visitors can soak in the charming ambiance and admire the traditional Provençal architecture. The village itself is characterised by narrow streets, quaint shops, and lovely squares.

Wine Production: Cassis is also renowned for its wine production. The region is known for producing high-quality white wines, especially the Cassis AOC (Appellation d'Origine Contrôlée) wines made from grapes grown on the limestone hillsides. Visitors can explore the local vineyards, taste the wines, and learn about the winemaking process.

Outdoor Activities: Apart from the calanques, Cassis offers a wide range of outdoor activities. Hiking enthusiasts can explore the numerous trails in the Calanques National Park, which offer breathtaking views of the coastline. Scuba diving and snorkelling are popular activities due to the clear waters and rich marine life.

Gastronomy: Cassis is a paradise for food lovers, with a wide range of restaurants and cafes offering delicious Provençal cuisine. Visitors can savour fresh seafood, local specialties like bouillabaisse (fish stew), and indulge in the famous wines of the region.

Overall, Cassis is a captivating destination that combines natural beauty, coastal charm, and a rich cultural heritage. Whether you're seeking relaxation on the beach, outdoor adventures, or culinary delights, Cassis has something to offer for everyone.

Saint-Paul-de-Vence: Art Lover's Haven

Saint-Paul-de-Vence is a charming mediaeval village located in the Provence-Alpes-Côte d'Azur region of southern France. It is renowned as an art lover's haven and attracts visitors from around the world. Here is some detailed and short information about Saint-Paul-de-Vence:

Location: Saint-Paul-de-Vence is perched on a hilltop about 15 kilometres inland from the French Riviera city of Nice. It is surrounded by picturesque landscapes, including rolling hills, vineyards, and olive groves.

Artistic Heritage: The village has a rich artistic heritage and has been a gathering place for artists and creative minds for decades. It has inspired many famous artists, including Marc Chagall, who lived and worked in Saint-Paul-de-Vence. The artistic ambiance is still evident today, with numerous galleries, art studios, and sculptures dotting the village.

Historic Village: Saint-Paul-de-Vence has a well-preserved mediaeval charm with its narrow, winding streets, ancient stone buildings, and fortified walls. The village is car-free, adding to its tranquil and timeless atmosphere. Visitors can explore the cobblestone streets, admire the beautiful architecture, and discover hidden squares and fountains.

Fondation Maeght: One of the main art attractions in Saint-Paul-de-Vence is the Fondation Maeght. This renowned modern art museum showcases an impressive collection of contemporary art, including works by artists like Joan Miró, Alexander Calder, and Alberto Giacometti. The museum also features a sculpture garden, offering a delightful blend of art and nature.

Art Galleries and Studios: Saint-Paul-de-Vence is home to numerous art galleries and studios, where visitors can discover a diverse range of artistic expressions. From traditional paintings to contemporary sculptures, the village offers a vibrant art scene that caters to all tastes and preferences.

Views and Vistas: The elevated position of Saint-Paul-de-Vence offers breathtaking panoramic views of the surrounding countryside, including the Mediterranean Sea in the distance. Visitors can enjoy stunning vistas from the village walls or from charming outdoor cafes and restaurants.

Dining and Shopping: Saint-Paul-de-Vence is a haven for food and shopping enthusiasts. The village boasts excellent restaurants that serve both traditional Provençal cuisine and innovative gastronomic creations. Visitors can also explore a variety of boutique shops, featuring local crafts, art, and unique souvenirs.

Events and Festivals: Throughout the year, Saint-Paul-de-Vence hosts various cultural events and festivals, celebrating art, music, and local traditions. These events often attract artists, performers, and visitors from near and far, adding an extra layer of excitement to the village's vibrant atmosphere.

In summary, Saint-Paul-de-Vence offers a captivating blend of history, art, and natural beauty. It is a haven for art enthusiasts, offering a wealth of galleries, museums, and an artistic ambiance that permeates the entire village. With its charming mediaeval setting, stunning views, and cultural events, Saint-Paul-de-Vence is a must-visit destination for anyone seeking a unique and inspiring experience in Provence.

Gordes: Panoramic Village Views

Gordes is a captivating hilltop village located in the Luberon region of Provence, France. It is renowned for its panoramic views, stunning architecture, and rich cultural heritage. Here is some detailed and short information about Gordes:

Location: Gordes is situated in the Vaucluse department of Provence, perched on a rocky outcrop overlooking the Luberon Valley. It is surrounded by beautiful landscapes, including vineyards, lavender fields, and olive groves.

Panoramic Views: One of the main attractions of Gordes is its breathtaking panoramic views. From the village, visitors can enjoy sweeping vistas of the Luberon Valley and the surrounding countryside, with its rolling hills and picturesque villages. The view is especially mesmerising at sunrise and sunset.

Architecture: Gordes is renowned for its distinctive architecture, characterised by stone houses and buildings that blend harmoniously with the natural landscape. The village is built in tiers, with narrow cobblestone streets, winding alleys, and charming squares. The iconic Gordes Castle, a Renaissance fortress, stands proudly at the top of the village and offers additional panoramic views.

Village Life: Gordes exudes a tranquil and authentic Provençal ambiance. The village is known for its traditional way of life, and visitors can immerse themselves in the local culture by exploring the weekly market, browsing through artisan shops, and sampling regional products like lavender honey and olive oil.

Historical Sites: Gordes boasts a rich historical heritage. Apart from the Gordes Castle, visitors can explore other historical sites such as the 12th-century Saint-Germain Abbey and the Romanesque Sénanque Abbey, located just outside the village. These sites provide insight into the village's mediaeval past and offer a glimpse into its religious and architectural history.

Art and Culture: Gordes has long been a haven for artists and creative individuals. The village is home to numerous art galleries, studios, and workshops where visitors can discover and appreciate local artwork. Gordes also hosts cultural events and festivals throughout the year, showcasing music, theatre, and traditional Provençal arts.

Outdoor Activities: The natural surroundings of Gordes offer ample opportunities for outdoor activities. Visitors can embark on scenic hikes through the Luberon Regional Nature Park, explore the nearby Sénanque Valley, or go cycling along picturesque country roads. The region is also known for its extensive network of walking trails that showcase the diverse landscapes.

Gastronomy: Gordes is a paradise for food enthusiasts, with a range of restaurants and cafes offering delicious Provençal cuisine. Visitors can savour traditional dishes like ratatouille, truffle-infused delicacies, and local cheeses, paired with renowned Luberon wines.

In summary, Gordes is a captivating village that combines stunning panoramic views, architectural beauty, and a rich cultural heritage. Whether you're exploring its historic sites, immersing yourself in the local way of life, or simply admiring the breathtaking vistas, Gordes offers a unique and unforgettable experience in the heart of Provence.

Antibes: History, Culture, and Beautiful Beaches

Antibes is a vibrant coastal town located in the Provence-Alpes-Côte d'Azur region of southern France. It offers a captivating blend of history, culture, and beautiful beaches. Here is some detailed and short information about Antibes:

Location: Antibes is situated between Nice and Cannes on the French Riviera, overlooking the Mediterranean Sea. Its prime coastal location makes it a popular destination for both locals and tourists.

History and Culture: Antibes has a rich history dating back to ancient times. The town was originally founded by the Greeks and later became a Roman colony. Throughout the centuries, Antibes has been influenced by various civilizations, including the Greeks, Romans, and even Napoleon Bonaparte. The historic old town, known as Vieil Antibes, still retains its mediaeval charm with narrow streets, ancient ramparts, and picturesque squares.

Fortifications and Museums: Antibes is famous for its impressive fortifications, particularly the Fort Carré, a star-shaped fortress that offers panoramic views of the town and coastline. The town also boasts several museums, including the Picasso Museum, located in the Château Grimaldi. This museum houses an extensive collection of Picasso's works, as the artist himself spent time in Antibes.

Port Vauban: Antibes is home to Port Vauban, one of the largest marinas in Europe. The port attracts luxury yachts and sailboats, adding to the town's glamorous allure. Visitors can stroll along the port, admire the impressive vessels, and enjoy the vibrant atmosphere of the waterfront cafes and restaurants.

Sandy Beaches: Antibes offers beautiful sandy beaches that stretch along the coastline. The most famous beach is Plage de la Gravette, located near the old town. It provides a picturesque setting for sunbathing and swimming. Other popular beaches include Plage du Ponteil and Plage de la Salis, both offering stunning views and crystal-clear waters.

Provençal Cuisine: Antibes is a paradise for food lovers, with a wide range of restaurants and cafes offering delicious Provençal cuisine. Visitors can indulge in fresh seafood, Mediterranean flavours, and regional specialties such as bouillabaisse (fish stew) and socca (a local chickpea pancake). The town is also known for its vibrant food markets, where visitors can sample and purchase local produce.

Events and Festivals: Antibes hosts various events and festivals throughout the year, adding to its lively cultural scene. The Jazz à Juan festival, held annually in July, attracts renowned jazz musicians from around the world. The Antibes Yacht Show and the Antibes Juan-les-Pins Jazz Festival are also popular events that draw crowds to the town.

Overall, Antibes offers a delightful mix of history, culture, and stunning beaches. Whether you're exploring its ancient streets, immersing yourself in art and museums, or simply enjoying the sun and sea, Antibes provides a memorable experience in the beautiful region of Provence.

Saintes-Maries-de-la-Mer: Gateway to the Camargue

Saintes-Maries-de-la-Mer is a charming coastal village located in the Camargue region of Provence, France. It serves as the gateway to the unique and picturesque Camargue, known for its natural beauty, wildlife, and rich cultural heritage. Here is some detailed and short information about Saintes-Maries-de-la-Mer:

Location: Saintes-Maries-de-la-Mer is situated on the Mediterranean coast in the southernmost part of Provence. It is nestled within the vast wetlands and marshes of the Camargue, between the Rhône River and the sea.

Camargue Natural Park: The village serves as the starting point to explore the Camargue Natural Park, a protected area known for its exceptional biodiversity. The park is home to diverse ecosystems, including salt marshes, lagoons, rice fields, and sandy beaches. It is renowned for its pink flamingos, wild horses, black bulls, and a variety of bird species.

Gypsy Pilgrimage: Saintes-Maries-de-la-Mer holds great significance for the Roma community and attracts thousands of pilgrims each year. According to legend, the town is associated with Saint Sarah, the patron saint of the Roma people. A famous pilgrimage, known as the "Pèlerinage des Gitans," takes place every May 24-25, drawing devotees who gather to honour Saint Sarah.

Beaches: The village offers beautiful sandy beaches that stretch along the Mediterranean coast. These beaches are popular for sunbathing, swimming, and water sports. Plage de l'Est, Plage de la Vierge, and Plage de Beauduc are among the most notable beaches in the area.

Cultural Heritage: Saintes-Maries-de-la-Mer has a rich cultural heritage that blends French, Spanish, and Roma influences. The village features traditional Camargue architecture with whitewashed buildings and colourful shutters. The Eglise des Saintes-Maries-de-la-Mer, a Romanesque church located in the town centre, is an important cultural and religious landmark.

Traditional Festivals: The village is known for its vibrant traditional festivals that showcase the local culture and traditions. The "Féria du Cheval" is an annual event in July that celebrates the Camargue's equestrian traditions with horse parades, bullfights, and traditional music. The "Fête des Saintes-Maries" is another notable festival held in late May, featuring processions, concerts, and traditional Provençal dances.

Wildlife and Nature: The Camargue is a paradise for nature lovers and birdwatchers. It is home to over 400 bird species, including flamingos, herons, egrets, and avocets. Visitors can explore the vast wetlands by foot, bike, or on horseback, and observe the rich flora and fauna that thrive in this unique environment.

Gastronomy: Saintes-Maries-de-la-Mer offers a variety of gastronomic delights, showcasing the flavours of the Camargue region. Visitors can enjoy traditional Camargue dishes such as gardiane de taureau (bull meat stew), fougasse (a regional bread), and delicious seafood dishes.

In summary, Saintes-Maries-de-la-Mer is a charming village that serves as the gateway to the captivating Camargue region. It offers a unique blend of natural beauty, wildlife, cultural heritage, and traditional festivals. Whether you're exploring the wetlands, enjoying the beaches, or immersing yourself in the local traditions, Saintes-Maries-de-la-Mer provides a memorable experience in the heart of Provence.

Itineraries

One Week Highlights and Hidden Gems

Provence is a beautiful region in southeastern France, known for its stunning landscapes, rich history, and vibrant culture. If you have one week to explore Provence, here are some highlights and hidden gems you shouldn't miss:

1. Avignon: Start your week in Avignon, a historic city famous for its well-preserved mediaeval architecture. Visit the Palais des Papes, a grand palace that was the seat of the Catholic popes in the 14th century. Take a stroll through the charming streets and visit the Pont d'Avignon, a bridge with a fascinating history.

2. Aix-en-Provence: Next, head to Aix-en-Provence, a picturesque town known for its elegant boulevards, stunning fountains, and vibrant arts scene. Explore the charming Old

Town, visit the famous Cours Mirabeau promenade, and don't miss the opportunity to see the birthplace of renowned painter Paul Cézanne.

3. Gorges du Verdon: Make your way to the breathtaking Gorges du Verdon, often referred to as the "Grand Canyon of Europe." Experience the stunning turquoise waters of the Verdon River as you hike along the rugged cliffs or rent a kayak for an unforgettable adventure.

4. Luberon Villages: Discover the hidden gems of the Luberon region by exploring its charming villages. Visit Gordes, a picturesque hilltop village with narrow streets and stunning views. Don't miss Roussillon, famous for its unique ochre cliffs and colourful houses, or Ménerbes, a quaint village known for its literary history.

5. Les Baux-de-Provence: Head to Les Baux-de-Provence, a mediaeval village perched on a rocky outcrop. Explore the narrow streets, visit the impressive Château des Baux, and enjoy panoramic views of the surrounding countryside.

6. Marseille: Spend a day in Marseille, France's second-largest city and a vibrant melting pot of cultures. Visit the historic Vieux-Port, explore the picturesque neighbourhood of Le Panier, and enjoy the Mediterranean atmosphere while indulging in delicious seafood cuisine.

7. Calanques National Park: End your week with a visit to the Calanques National Park, a natural wonder characterised by dramatic limestone cliffs and crystal-clear turquoise waters. Take a boat tour or hike along the coastal trails to admire the stunning calanques (narrow, steep-walled inlets) and enjoy the pristine beaches.

These are just a few highlights and hidden gems that Provence has to offer. The region is full of charming towns, picturesque landscapes, and cultural treasures, so take the time to explore and immerse yourself in the beauty and authenticity of this captivating region.

Family-Friendly Adventure

Provence in France offers numerous family-friendly adventures that combine outdoor activities, cultural experiences, and opportunities for relaxation. Here is some detailed and concise information on planning a family-friendly adventure in Provence:

1. Camargue Nature Reserve: Explore the Camargue, a unique wetland region known for its diverse wildlife. Take a guided safari tour to spot flamingos, white horses, and black bulls in their natural habitats. Kids will love the opportunity to see these magnificent creatures up close.

2. Aqua Splash: Visit Aqua Splash, a water park located in the town of Monteux. It offers a variety of water slides, pools, and play areas suitable for all ages. Spend a fun-filled day enjoying the attractions and cooling off from the summer heat.

3. Arles: Discover the ancient Roman city of Arles, which offers a range of family-friendly activities. Visit the Arles Amphitheatre, where gladiator

battles once took place, and explore the Roman Theater. The Van Gogh Foundation is also worth a visit, showcasing the works of the famous painter who was inspired by the region.

4. Tree-Top Adventure Parks: Try out tree-top adventure parks such as Forest Adventure in Salon-de-Provence or Accro Passion in La Colle-sur-Loup. These parks feature ziplines, rope courses, and obstacle courses at varying difficulty levels, providing a thrilling experience for both children and adults.

5. Lavender Fields: Take a trip to the stunning lavender fields in Provence, especially during the blooming season (typically June to August). Kids will enjoy running through the fragrant fields and capturing beautiful family photos amidst the vibrant purple hues.

6. Marseille's Old Port: Visit Marseille's Old Port, a bustling waterfront area with numerous family-friendly attractions. Take a boat tour to see the coastline, visit the interactive Museum of European and Mediterranean Civilizations

(MUCEM), and enjoy a delicious seafood lunch at one of the many waterfront restaurants.

7. Gorges du Verdon: Embark on a family adventure to the Gorges du Verdon, where you can hike, bike, or kayak amidst the stunning turquoise waters and towering cliffs. For a more relaxed experience, take a boat tour and admire the breathtaking scenery together.

8. Beaches: Enjoy some quality family time at the beaches of Provence. Prado Beach in Marseille and Plage de l'Espiguette in the Camargue are popular choices, offering sandy shores, shallow waters, and facilities for water sports and picnics.

Remember to plan your itinerary based on the ages and interests of your family members, ensuring a balance between adventure, relaxation, and cultural exploration. Provence provides a diverse range of activities that will create lasting memories for everyone in the family.

Romantic Retreat: Enchanting Places

Provence in France is renowned for its romantic atmosphere, picturesque landscapes, and charming villages, making it an ideal destination for a romantic retreat. Here is some detailed and concise information on enchanting places in Provence for a romantic getaway:

1. Gordes: Located in the Luberon region, Gordes is a captivating hilltop village known for its stunning views and mediaeval architecture. Stroll hand in hand through its narrow streets, visit the 12th-century castle, and enjoy a romantic dinner at one of the village's intimate restaurants.

2. Isle-sur-la-Sorgue: This charming town is often referred to as the "Venice of Provence" due to its canals and waterwheels. Explore the romantic waterways, browse through the antique shops and art galleries, and share a romantic picnic by the river.

3. Saint-Rémy-de-Provence: Surrounded by beautiful landscapes, Saint-Rémy-de-Provence is an idyllic town that inspired renowned artists like Van Gogh. Take a leisurely walk through the cobbled streets, visit the Saint-Paul-de-Mausole monastery, and savour a romantic dinner at one of the cosy Provençal restaurants.

4. Valensole Plateau: The Valensole Plateau is famous for its sprawling lavender fields, creating a romantic and fragrant backdrop. Plan your visit during the lavender blooming season (June to August) to witness the breathtaking purple hues and enjoy a romantic stroll through the fields.

5. Cassis: Nestled between towering cliffs and the Mediterranean Sea, Cassis is a picturesque fishing village known for its charming harbour and pristine beaches. Take a boat trip to explore the nearby Calanques, enjoy a sunset walk along the waterfront, and savour fresh seafood together.

6. Aix-en-Provence: The elegant town of Aix-en-Provence exudes a romantic ambiance with its tree-lined streets, beautiful squares, and

vibrant café culture. Explore the historic Old Town hand in hand, visit the Cours Mirabeau promenade, and indulge in a couple's spa treatment at one of the luxurious wellness centres.

7. Châteauneuf-du-Pape: For wine-loving couples, Châteauneuf-du-Pape is a must-visit destination. This charming village is renowned for its world-class vineyards and wine production. Take a wine tour, sample exquisite wines together, and enjoy a romantic picnic among the vineyards.

8. Pont du Gard: Visit the awe-inspiring Pont du Gard, an ancient Roman aqueduct bridge that spans the Gardon River. Admire the architectural marvel, take a romantic walk along the riverbanks, and have a picnic with a view of the bridge.

Provence offers a multitude of enchanting places that are perfect for a romantic retreat. Whether you prefer strolling through charming villages, exploring natural landscapes, or savouring fine wine and cuisine, Provence has something to offer every romantic couple.

Off-the-Beaten-Path Exploration

If you're looking to explore off-the-beaten-path destinations in Provence, here is some detailed and concise information on unique and lesser-known places to discover:

1. Séguret: Tucked away in the Vaucluse region, Séguret is a charming hilltop village that offers a glimpse into mediaeval Provence. With its narrow streets, stone houses, and panoramic views of the surrounding vineyards, it provides a tranquil and authentic atmosphere away from the crowds.

2. Moustiers-Sainte-Marie: Located near the stunning Gorges du Verdon, Moustiers-Sainte-Marie is a hidden gem known for its picturesque setting and traditional ceramics. Explore the narrow streets adorned with vibrant flower pots, visit the Notre-Dame-de-Beauvoir chapel perched on a hill, and admire the cascading waterfall that flows through the village.

3. Les Baux-de-Provence Carrières de Lumières: Discover an extraordinary art exhibition at the Carrières de Lumières, a former limestone quarry turned immersive multimedia space. Walk through the cavernous chambers where famous artworks are projected onto the walls, creating a mesmerising visual experience.

4. Forcalquier: Situated in the Alpes-de-Haute-Provence department, Forcalquier is a charming Provençal town off the tourist trail. Visit the 13th-century citadel, explore the traditional market, and enjoy the tranquil atmosphere while wandering through its mediaeval streets.

5. L'Isle-sur-la-Sorgue Antique Market: If you're a fan of antiques and vintage treasures, head to L'Isle-sur-la-Sorgue on a Sunday morning. This small town transforms into a bustling antique market, with vendors showcasing their unique finds. Browse through the stalls, hunt for hidden gems, and enjoy the lively atmosphere.

6. Abbaye Notre-Dame de Sénanque: Tucked away in a picturesque valley near Gordes, the Abbaye Notre-Dame de Sénanque is a stunning Cistercian abbey dating back to the 12th century. Surrounded by lavender fields, it offers a serene and photogenic setting, especially during the blooming season.

7. Gorges de la Nesque: For a scenic drive or bike ride, venture into the Gorges de la Nesque. This lesser-known gorge offers breathtaking views of the rugged cliffs, winding roads, and the Nesque River. Stop at the viewpoints along the way to admire the stunning landscapes.

8. Ventabren: Perched on a hilltop overlooking the Etang de Berre, Ventabren is a charming Provençal village with a rich history. Wander through its mediaeval streets, visit the ruins of the Château de Ventabren, and enjoy panoramic views of the surrounding countryside.

Exploring these off-the-beaten-path destinations in Provence will allow you to experience the region's hidden treasures, discover lesser-known gems, and create unique memories during your journey.

Conclusion: Departing with Lasting Memories

As your journey in Provence comes to a close, departing with lasting memories is inevitable. Here's some detailed and concise information on the essence of your experience and the impressions that will stay with you:

1. Captivating Landscapes: The breathtaking landscapes of Provence, from rolling lavender fields to dramatic cliffs and azure coastlines, will leave an indelible mark. The vibrant colours, scents, and sheer beauty of the region's natural surroundings will remain etched in your memory.

2. Charming Villages: The enchanting Provençal villages with their narrow cobblestone streets, charming squares, and historic architecture will evoke a sense of timeless beauty. The warmth of the locals and the intimate atmosphere of these villages will be fondly remembered.

3. Rich History: Provence's rich historical heritage, including Roman ruins, mediaeval castles, and ancient abbey sites, will leave you with a deeper appreciation for the region's cultural significance. The stories and narratives that unfold through these historical landmarks will stay with you.

4. Gastronomic Delights: The delectable cuisine and exquisite wines of Provence will linger in your taste buds long after you leave. The flavours of fresh produce, fragrant herbs, olive oil, and regional specialties like bouillabaisse will remind you of the culinary delights you savoured during your stay.

5. Artistic Inspirations: Provence has inspired numerous artists throughout history, and the artistic legacy of the region is palpable. The brushstrokes of Van Gogh, the writings of Cézanne, and the melodic notes of traditional Provençal music will resonate within you, leaving a lasting artistic impression.

6. Timeless Provencal Lifestyle: The relaxed and unhurried pace of life in Provence will be a

cherished memory. The joy of savouring long meals, engaging in leisurely strolls, and embracing the art of "joie de vivre" will be a reminder of the region's timeless lifestyle.

7. Personal Connections: The connections made with locals, fellow travellers, and the welcoming Provençal people will leave a lasting impact. The shared moments, conversations, and cultural exchanges will be treasured memories of your time in Provence.

As you depart from Provence, these lasting memories will serve as a reminder of the region's beauty, charm, and cultural richness. The experiences and impressions gained during your visit will continue to inspire and captivate, keeping the spirit of Provence alive within you.

APPRECIATION

Dear valued customers,

We would like to take a moment to express our heartfelt appreciation to each and every one of you who has chosen to purchase the Provence Travel Guide 2023 by Silva Martin. Your support and trust mean the world to us.

We understand that selecting a travel guide is an important decision, and we are honoured that you have chosen ours to accompany you on your journey through the beautiful region of Provence. We have poured our passion, knowledge, and expertise into creating a comprehensive and engaging guide that we hope will enhance your travel experience.

Through this guide, we aim to provide you with insightful recommendations, hidden gems, historical insights, and practical information to make your visit to Provence truly memorable. We want to empower you to explore the picturesque landscapes, discover charming towns, indulge in exquisite cuisine, and immerse yourself in the rich culture that Provence has to offer.

Your decision to support our work not only enables us to continue producing high-quality travel guides but also encourages us to constantly improve and strive for excellence. We value your feedback, suggestions, and experiences, as they help us refine our offerings and ensure that future travellers have an even better experience.

We hope that the Provence Travel Guide 2023 becomes your trusted companion during your adventures, providing you with inspiration, guidance, and unforgettable moments. May it open doors to new discoveries, spark your curiosity, and create lasting memories that you will cherish for a lifetime.

Once again, thank you for choosing the Provence Travel Guide 2023. We wish you an incredible journey through the enchanting landscapes of Provence and hope that this guide becomes an indispensable part of your travel experience.

Warm regards,

The Silva Martin Team

Printed in Great Britain
by Amazon

25621301R00119